25 OF YOUR FAVORITE DINOSAURS
TO FOLD IN AN INSTANT

DINOGAMI

MARI ONO & HIROAKI TAKAI

CICO BOOKS
LONDON NEW YORK

Published in 2012 by CICO Books
An imprint of Ryland Peters & Small Ltd
20–21 Jockey's Fields 519 Broadway, 5th Floor
London WC1R 4BW New York, NY 10012

www.cicobooks.com

10 9 8 7 6 5 4

Text © Mari Ono and Hiroaki Takai 2012
Design and photography © CICO Books
2012

A CIP catalog record for this book is
available from the Library of Congress
and the British Library.

ISBN: 978 1 908170 95 8

Printed in China

Editor: Robin Gurdon
Designer: Jerry Goldie
Photographer: Geoff Dann
Photography styling, set design,
and illustration: Trina Dalziel

For digital editions, visit www.cicobooks.com/apps.php

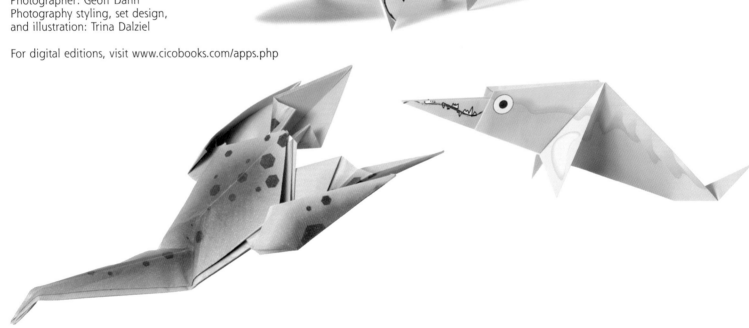

CONTENTS

INTRODUCTION

Welcome to *Dinogami*! Hiroaki Takai and I have worked together to create these fun paper dinosaurs for you to make. Hiroaki is one of Japan's *origami* masters who every day design wonderful new models to put a smile on the faces of the people who make them. The tradition of the *origami* master dates back over 1000 years, and they have passed down paper-folding techniques from generation to generation, influencing a new breed of *origami* fans who are creating exciting new models like the dinosaurs in this book.

To start your own quest to become an *origami* master, you need to be challenged, and that's what these 25 dinosaurs aim to do. Begin with a simple project and learn a few basic folds before moving on to something a bit more ambitious. You'll soon find yourself picking up the skills that Japanese people have been using for centuries and making models that even *origami* masters would be proud of.

One of the best things about *origami* is that it stimulates the mind and allows you to create something with your hands, but the most important aspect is that it is great fun and we hope you will enjoy bringing the models to life.

MARI ONO

BASIC TECHNIQUES

Origami is a very simple craft that anyone from the smallest child upward can master. All that is required is a steady hand and some patience. Before you start making your first model just check over these simple tips to ensure every paper model you make is a success.

MAKING FOLDS

Making the paper fold as crisply and evenly as possible is the key to making models that will fly as the designs intend—it really is as simple as that.

1 When you make a fold ensure that the paper lies exactly where you want it, with the corners sitting exactly on top of each other.

2 As you make the crease be sure to keep the paper completely still so that the fold is perfectly true and straight.

3 Still holding the paper with your spare hand use a ruler or perhaps the side of a pencil to press down the fold until it is as flat as possible.

OPENING FOLDS

Sometimes you will need to open out a crease and refold the paper so that it lies in a new shape, as in the triangle fold shown here.

1 Lift the flap to be opened out and begin pulling the two sides apart.

2 As the space widens you will need to be sure that the far point folds true, so use a pencil to gently prise the paper open.

3 As the two corners separate the top point drops forward and the two edges open out to become one.

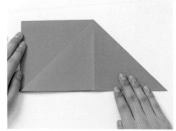

4 Press down the new creases to make the two new angled sides of the triangle.

REVERSING FOLDS

To reverse a crease you will need to open out your model and gently turn part of the paper back on itself. This can sometimes be tricky so practice on an old model first.

1 To turn the tip back on itself first make a firm crease with a simple fold.

2 Return the tip back to its original position and open out the model. Turn back the nose again along the fold you just made.

3 When you close the model together again the tip has reversed and is now flat.

KEY TO ARROWS

OPEN OUT
Open out and refold the paper over in the direction shown.

TURN OVER
Turn the paper over.

FOLD
Fold the part of the paper shown in this direction.

CHANGE THE POSITION
Spin the paper 90° in the direction of the arrows.

MAKE A CREASE
Fold the paper over in the direction of the arrow then open it out again.

FOLDING DIRECTION
Fold the entire paper over in this direction.

CHANGE THE POSITION
Spin the paper through 180°.

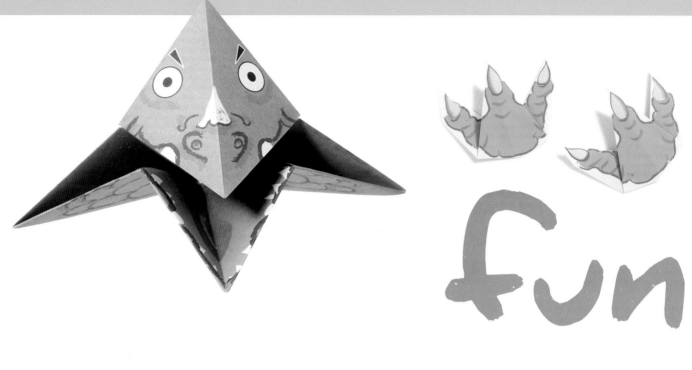

fun

DINOSAURS

01 ANCHICERATOPS

Anchiceratops, whose name means "horned face," lived in North America around 72 million years ago. Its skull included a big shield that protected the upper part of the head, as well as a pair of tough horns. This dinosaur is made using a traditional Japanese origami *fukusuke* model—when you are finished open his mouth and see how much he looks like a dinosaur.

You will need:
One sheet of 6 in (15 cm) square paper

1 With the design face down, fold the paper from corner to corner to make a crease and open, then repeat across the other corners. Next fold the corners in so that they meet at the center. Fold the corners in once more.

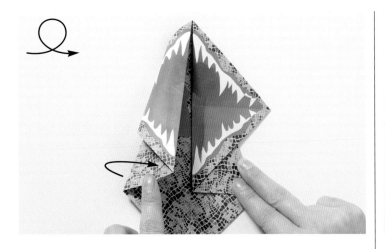

2 Turn the paper over and fold in the outer points so that the edges run down the middle of the model. Lift the model and allow the loose flaps to lie flat on top.

3 Turn over the top of the model, making the fold line across the widest part of the piece, and let the top flap out from behind the model.

FUN DINOSAURS

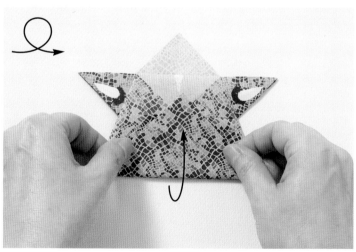

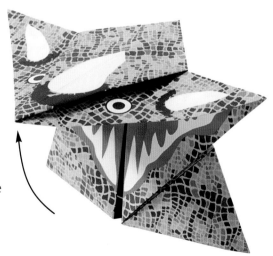

4 Turn the model over and fold up the loose flap then slightly open the side flaps at the back to allow the dinosaur to stand up.

02 ANKYLOSAURUS

Ankylosaurus was a very famous armored dinosaur that was known for its crocodile-like plates and the heavy club at the end of its tail. It was also one of the last dinosaurs of any type to live. Use two sheets of origami paper for this model; the body is made using the traditional Japanese design for a ship while the legs are made using the candy-holding bento box design.

You will need:
Two sheets of 6 in (15 cm) square paper

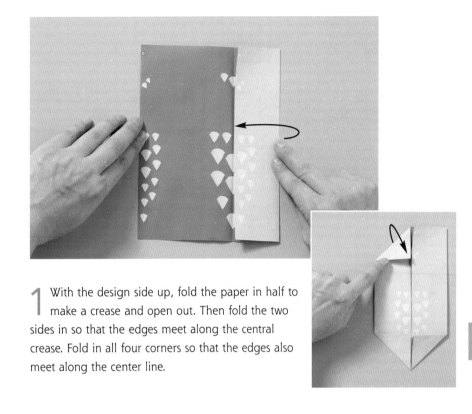

1 With the design side up, fold the paper in half to make a crease and open out. Then fold the two sides in so that the edges meet along the central crease. Fold in all four corners so that the edges also meet along the center line.

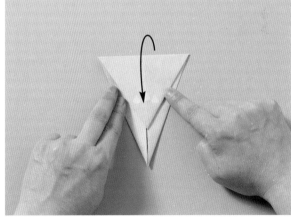

13

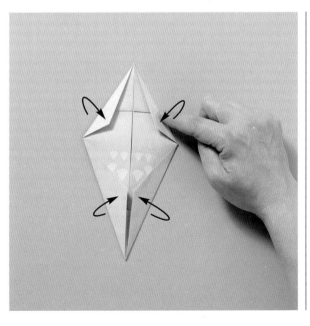

2 Fold up the bottom diagonal edges so that they meet along the center line. Then turn over the top diagonal edges, making folds from the upper point to the top of the folds just made.

3 Turn down the top point, making the horizontal fold between the widest points of the object.

ANKYLOSAURUS

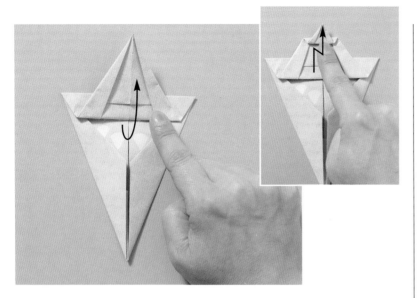

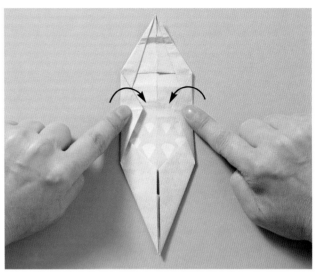

4 Fold back the top flap, making a fold about ½ in (1 cm) from the original fold, then make a second concertina fold about ½ in (1 cm) from the tip.

5 Open out the two concertina folds and turn in the outer points, making sure that the top of each fold is in line with the horizontal edge visible inside the object.

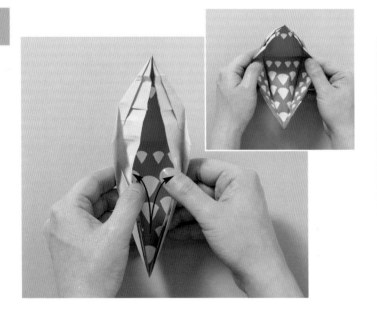

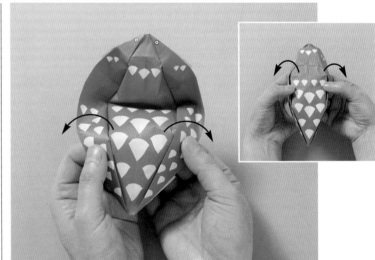

6 Now turn the whole model inside out by lifting the object and placing your thumbs on the edges running down the center of the object, then begin pulling them apart. As the edges diverge push the back forward with your little fingers.

7 Begin to reverse the long creases down the length of the model. When complete gently reverse the shorter creases at the top of the model taking care not to tear the edge of the origami paper. Finish by forming the shape with a flat back.

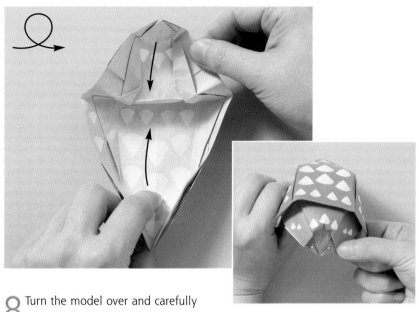

8 Turn the model over and carefully push the shorter end back on itself using the concertina creases made earlier. Finally use the smaller second set of concertina creases to push back the face and form the cheeks.

9 Take the second sheet of paper and with the design face down, fold the paper from corner to corner and open to make a crease then repeat across the other corners. Next fold the corners in so that they meet at the center.

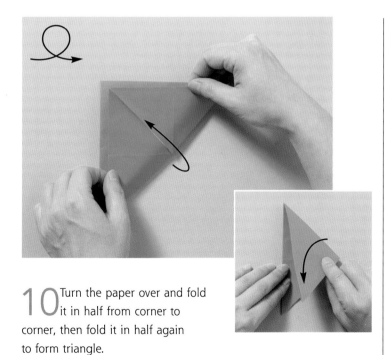

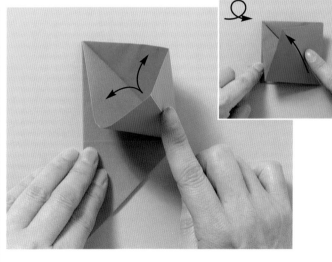

10 Turn the paper over and fold it in half from corner to corner, then fold it in half again to form triangle.

11 Lift the top flap then push the tip down towards the far point. Flatten the paper to form a diamond. Turn over and repeat, lifting the flap and pressing down into a triangle.

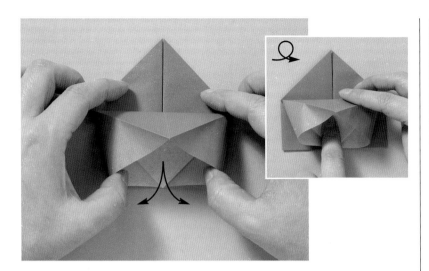

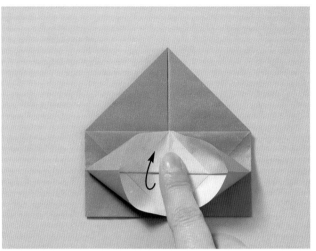

12 Spin the object so that the central line is vertical. Lift the top flap and put your thumbs inside, pulling the sides apart so that the tip flattens into an edge that ends up horizontally across the bottom of the object. Turn over and repeat.

13 Lift the bottom edge and fold it back to sit on the crease running across the middle of the object. Flatten the sides into triangles as you do this. Turn over and repeat.

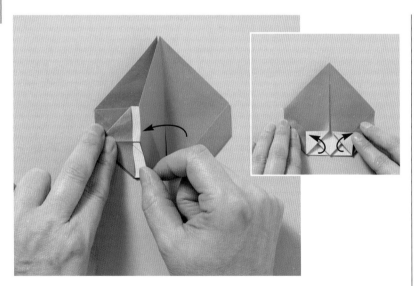

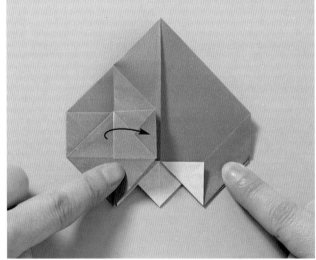

14 Turn the right-hand upper flap over to the left then turn the object over and repeat. Now turn over the bottom corners of the flaps that meet in the center of the object, making diagonal angles. Again, turn over and repeat.

15 Fold the upper flap on the left in so that the edge runs down the center of the object. Repeat on the right-hand side then turn the model over and repeat.

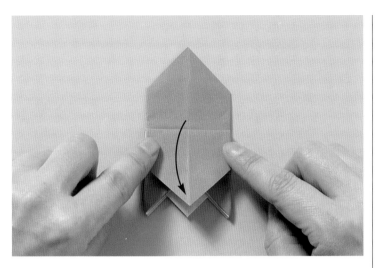

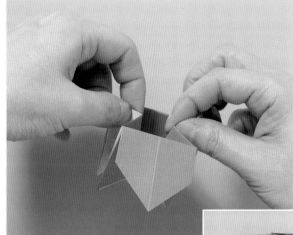

16 Fold down the top tip across the central crease so that the point sits on the bottom point. Turn over and repeat.

17 Lift up the paper and gently prise it open to form a square box. When it is formed fold the flaps back inside to form the dinosaur's legs.

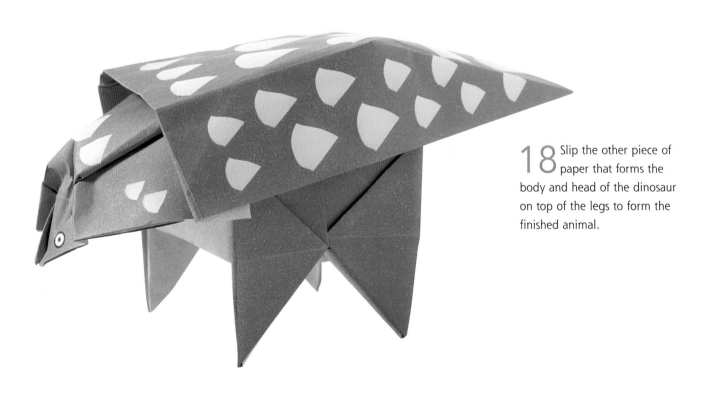

18 Slip the other piece of paper that forms the body and head of the dinosaur on top of the legs to form the finished animal.

03 VELOCIRAPTOR

Velociraptor became famous as the fleet-footed dinosaur with massive claws in the film *Jurassic Park*. Lately, though, velociraptor fossils with traces of feathers have been discovered in China, fueling the theory of these "feathered dinosaurs" being related to birds. As you make this model take care to fold all the creases firmly to create the perfect shape.

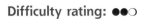
You will need:
Two sheets of 6 in (15 cm) square paper

1 With the design face down, fold the paper from corner to corner both ways and from side to side both ways. Open out, turn over and fold the sides into the center.

2 Fold in top and bottom edges to meet in the center then lift each flap, pushing out the corners and refold to make triangles on each side.

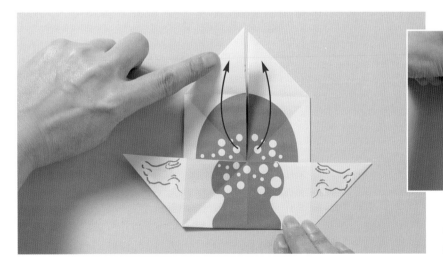

3 Turn the top two flaps up so the points meet at the top of the object then turn them down at an angle so that the whole shape of each foot is showing.

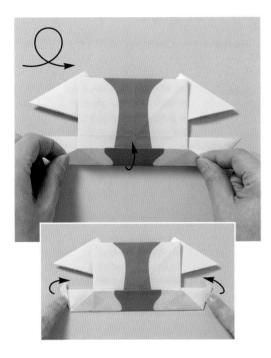

4 Turn over the paper and fold up the bottom edge so that it runs across the central crease then turn up the two outer points.

5 Take the second sheet and, design side down, fold it in half then open out and fold from corner to corner through the middle of the design.

6 Open out the paper and fold in the right-hand corner so that it sits on the first crease made in the previous step and the edge of the paper runs up to the top point. Turn the opposite point in so that the edges of the paper meet.

7 Fold over the left-hand side of the paper so that the edge runs down the central crease.

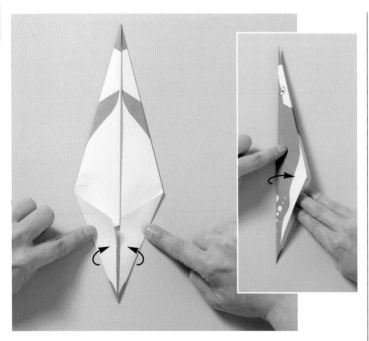

8 Fold in the bottom two edges so that they also meet along the central crease then fold the paper in half.

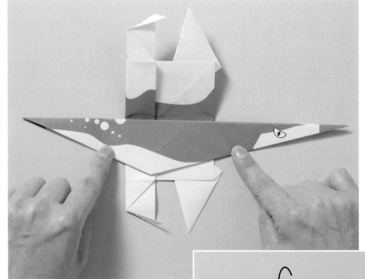

9 Place the second sheet on top of the first as shown and close the dinosaur's body around its neck and head.

10 Fold the dinosaur's neck back across the edge of its body and make a firm crease, then release. Make a second fold by turning the head up along the edge of the body.

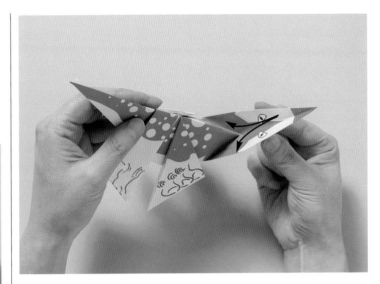

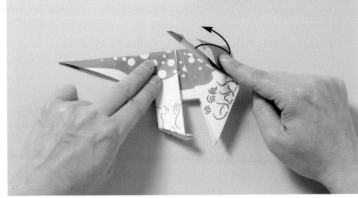

11 Lift the object up and gently open it out, reversing the folds so that the head sits vertically and inside-out.

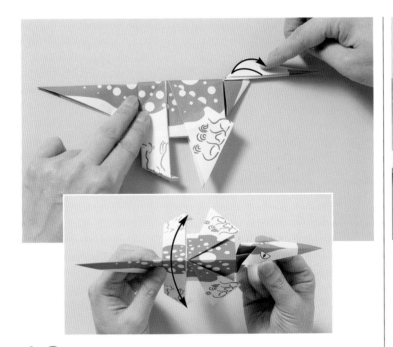

12 Fold the neck forward along the top of the dinosaur's body then lift the paper up again and reverse the folds, opening out the head and creating a neck.

13 Turn back the tip of the nose and push it inside the head to form a flat snout, and then prise down the tip to form the tongue.

04 DINOSAUR FOOTPRINTS

Have you ever found the fossil of a dinosaur's footprints? If not make a pair from a single sheet of origami paper which you can then place anywhere in the house and imagine the huge beast walking past. After cutting the design of the footprints in half with a pair of scissors, it will just take a couple of easy folds to make your very own "dinosaur footprints".

Difficulty rating: ●○○

You will need:
One sheet of 6 in (15 cm) square paper
Scissors

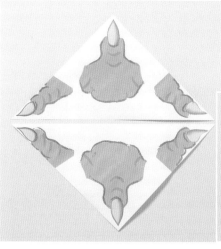

1 Cut the paper in half from corner to corner between the two designs then fold each one in half, making a crease down the middle of the paper.

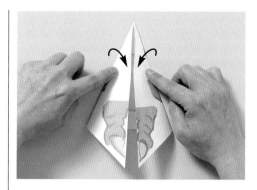

2 Open out the paper and fold the two side points down so that the edges of the paper meet along the center line.

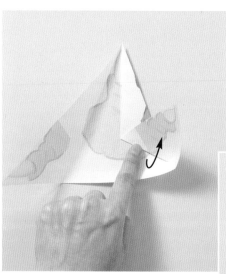

3 Fold back the right-hand point at an angle and press down so the corner of the paper lifts up. Press this down making a crease stretching most of the way across the model.

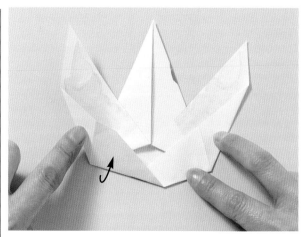

4 Repeat on the left-hand side to finish the footprint.

05 GIGANTOSAURUS

Gigantosaurus, which means "great lizard," has now been recognized as the largest of all the carnivorous dinosaurs, measuring a total of 13 to 15 meters. Just its face alone was the size of an adult human. Recreate the fierce face in origami then, once completed, move it by inserting your fingers into the back of its mouth—don't forget to roar as you play!

You will need:
One sheet of A5 (8¼ x 6 in/21 x 15 cm) paper

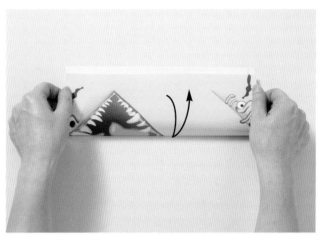

1 Fold the paper, with the design side face down, in half along its length to make a crease.

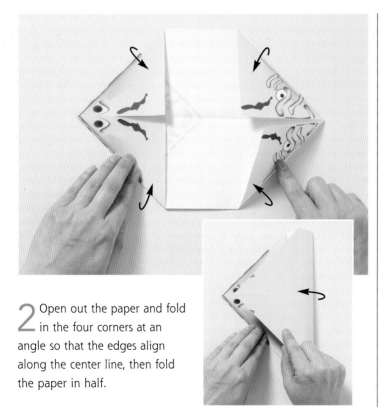
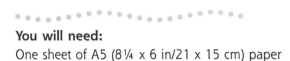

2 Open out the paper and fold in the four corners at an angle so that the edges align along the center line, then fold the paper in half.

3 Fold in the top and bottom corners so that they also meet along the center line then turn the object over and open the model's mouth to finish.

06 SCUTOSAURUS

Scutosaurus, meaning "shield reptile," was an armor-covered dinosaur that lived in Russia in the later Permian period. Its name comes from the latin for the large plates of armor scattered across its body—including its cheekbones, which were particularly large. This origami model is made using one of the traditional Japanese origami toy designs.

You will need:
One sheet of 6 in (15 cm) square paper

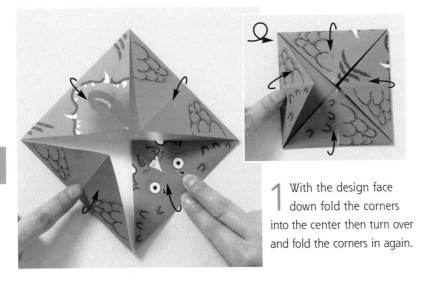

1 With the design face down fold the corners into the center then turn over and fold the corners in again.

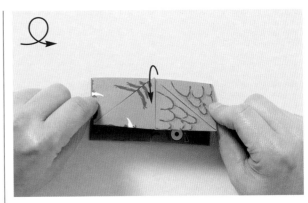

2 Turn the paper over and fold forward the top edge of the paper along the center line.

3 Lift the right-hand side then press the point forward, refolding the flap into a triangle. Turn over and repeat.

4 Lift up the paper and let the model open out slightly.

5 Press back the head from
the point at the top,
making a crease across its
widest part and letting the
lower flap come out. Fold
forward the remaining two
flaps to form the base for
the head.

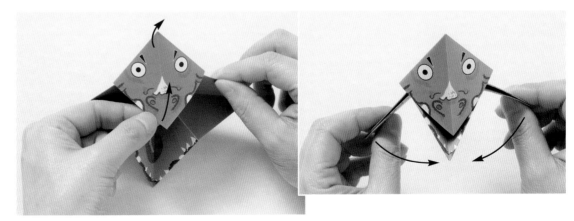

big DINOSAURS

07 APATOSAURUS

Huge and harmless, the apatosaurus was once more commonly known as the brontosaurus. Although this dinosaur weighed around 23 tons and was 23 meters long it spent its days gently eating as much vegetation as possible. Your model won't be so greedy but it will still be impressive.

1 To make the rear of the dinosaur, fold the sheet of paper without the eyes from corner to corner, then open out and fold in the other direction. Open out again and fold the two sides in so that the bottom edges meet along the center line.

You will need:
Two sheets of 6 in (15 cm) square paper

BIG DINOSAURS

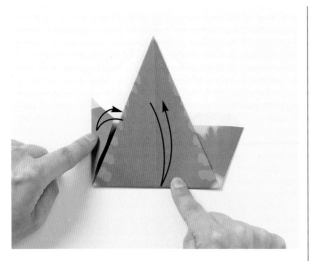

2 Fold the bottom point up to the top then fold in the two side points so that the edges run along the sides of the flap.

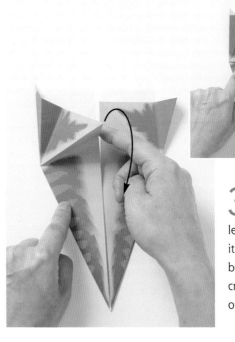

3 Open out the three folds made in the previous step, then lift the left-hand flap by the corner and turn it down so that the diagonal crease becomes the horizontal and a new crease is formed underneath. Repeat on the right-hand side.

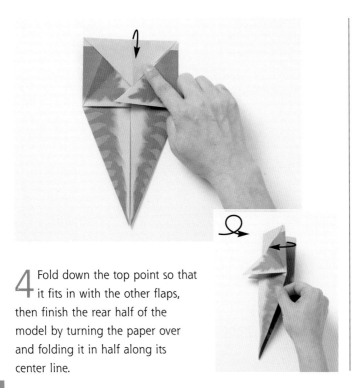

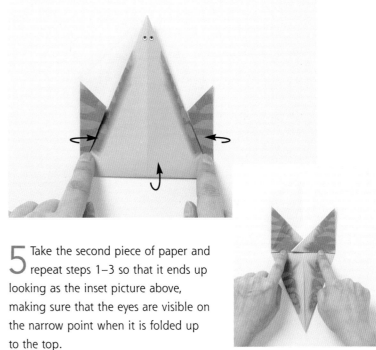

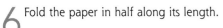**4** Fold down the top point so that it fits in with the other flaps, then finish the rear half of the model by turning the paper over and folding it in half along its center line.

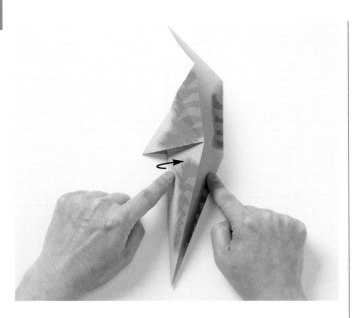

5 Take the second piece of paper and repeat steps 1–3 so that it ends up looking as the inset picture above, making sure that the eyes are visible on the narrow point when it is folded up to the top.

6 Fold the paper in half along its length.

7 Spin the paper through 90° and make a diagonal crease across the neck by turning up the long point so that its bottom edge runs up the side of the triangular flap.

8 Gently open out the paper and push the right-hand end back inside the body, reversing the creases so that it now points up at an angle.

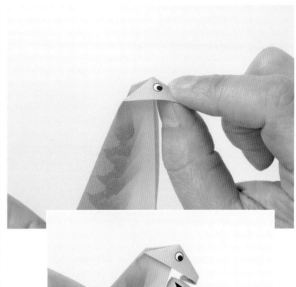

9 Turn over the tip of the nose, making sure that the fold is far enough along that the eyes will become visible in the next step.

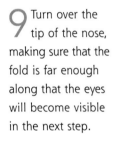

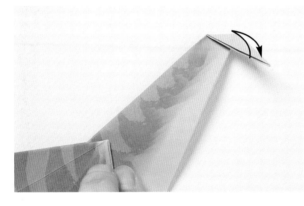

10 Open out the end of the neck and turn over the tip, reversing the crease just made to form the head. Turn the very end inside the flap to form a flat snout.

11 Slide the two sheets of paper together so that the front of the back section slides inside the folds of the diagonal flaps.

12 Turn over the top corners of the front flaps to hold the two sheets together.

08 ROCCOSAURUS

Roccosaurus was a large, herbivorous sauropod that lived in South Africa. Although by nature very quiet, if he was attacked by a carnivorous dinosaur he always fought fiercely to protect himself and the rest of his large herd. If you want to make more models than with just the origami paper attached, use rectangular sheets of paper to make models of different sizes.

You will need:
One sheet of A5 (8¼ x 6 in/21 x 15 cm) paper

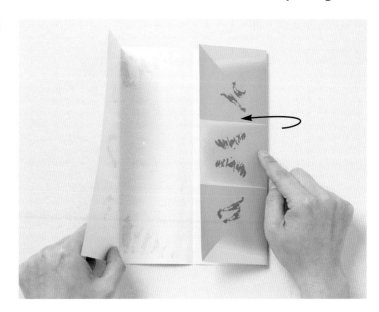

1 Fold the sheet in half widthways to make a crease, then open out and fold the sides in to meet in the middle.

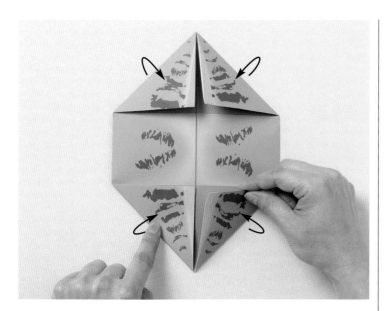

2 Fold in all four corners at an angle so that the edges meet along the center line.

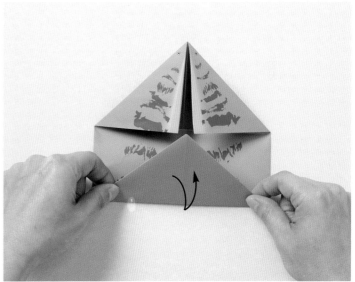

3 Make a horizontal crease by folding up the bottom across the edge of the flaps. Repeat at the top of the model.

4 Open out the four flaps and then lift the top right corner, opening out the flap and refolding it to form a triangle. Repeat on the left-hand side.

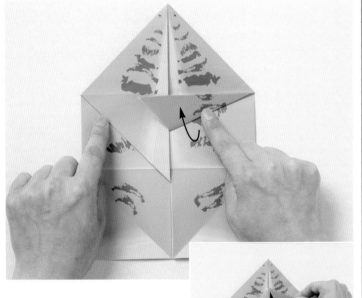

5 Fold up the bottom tip of the right-hand triangle so that the diagonal edge now runs across the piece, then fold the whole flap upwards.

6 Fold forward the shorter diagonal edge of the flap so that it runs horizontally along the same crease line, then turn the whole flap down.

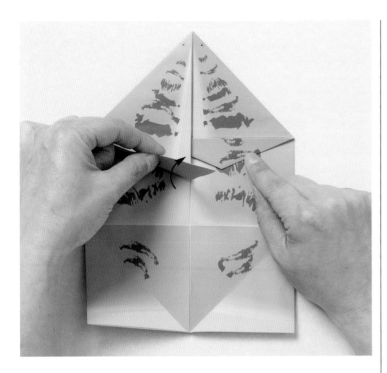

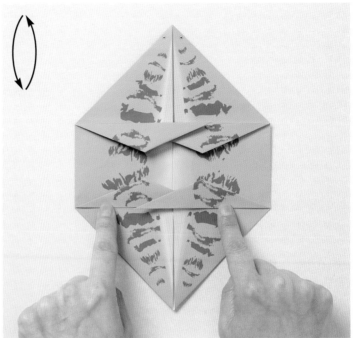

7 Tuck the end just created behind the opposite flap and repeat the previous two steps on the other side.

8 Now spin the paper through 180° and repeat the previous four steps at the other end.

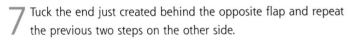

9 Turn the paper over and fold the top right-hand side over so that the diagonal edge runs down the center line. Repeat on all three other sides.

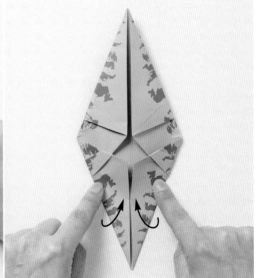

10 Lift the bottom right flap and then open out the folds inside, reversing the creases before folding back flat.

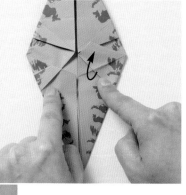

11 Prepare to fold the model in half by raising the new flap, using the short diagonal crease.

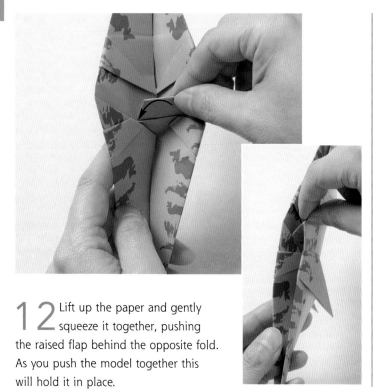

12 Lift up the paper and gently squeeze it together, pushing the raised flap behind the opposite fold. As you push the model together this will hold it in place.

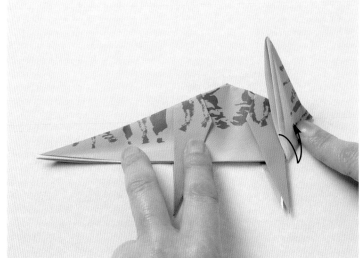

13 Fold the head back at an angle across the front legs to make a crease.

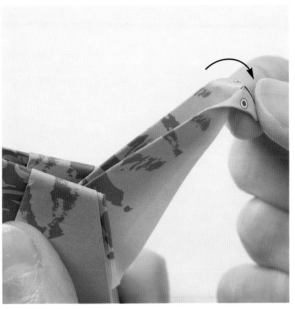

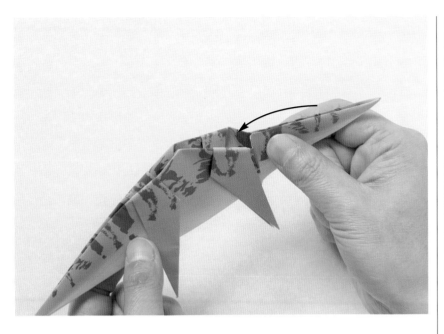

14 Gently open out the paper and push the right-hand end back inside the body, reversing the creases so that it now points up at an angle.

15 Make an angled crease across the end of the neck then open it out and reverse the folds to create the head, ensuring that the eyes are visible.

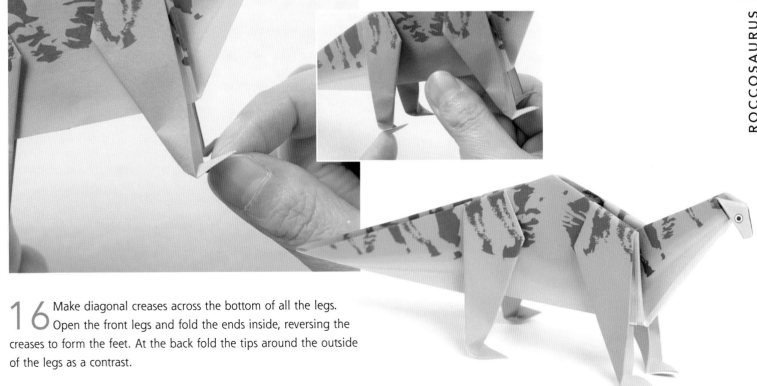

16 Make diagonal creases across the bottom of all the legs. Open the front legs and fold the ends inside, reversing the creases to form the feet. At the back fold the tips around the outside of the legs as a contrast.

09 BRACHIOSAURUS

Brachiosaurus is the largest and heaviest land animal that has ever been discovered. This massive dinosaur was 30 meters long and weighed over 70 tons. It was different from other large, plant-eating sauropods in a few key ways, with longer forelegs than hind legs and a long, more upright neck. These helped it eat the highest branches and made it look a bit like a huge giraffe.

You will need:
Two sheets of 6 in (15 cm) square paper

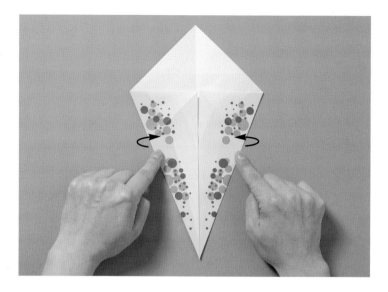

1 Make the rear of the dinosaur from the sheet without the eyes. Fold it in half from corner to corner both ways then open out and fold the bottom edges in to meet along the center line.

2 Fold up the bottom to meet the top point to make a crease, then fold in the side points so that the edges run along the edge of the flap.

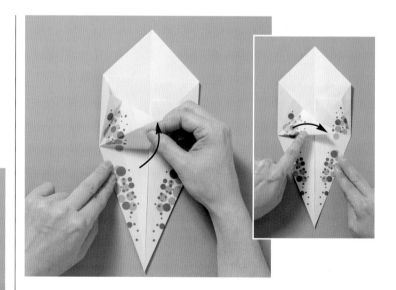

3 Open out the creases then lift the corner of the left-hand flap, opening out and reversing the folds so that it forms a triangle with a horizontal base. Repeat on the other side.

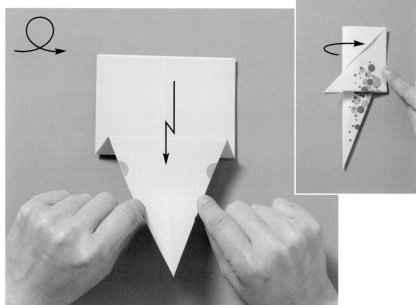

4 Fold down the top point so that the edges run alongside the existing flaps.

5 Turn the paper over and fold the bottom tip back across the horizontal crease before turning back the tip about ½ in (1 cm) from the fold. Now fold in half lengthways.

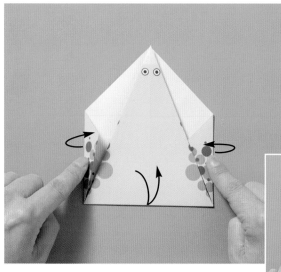

6 Take the second sheet of paper and follow steps 1–4, ensuring that the eyes are visible at the end of the narrow point.

7 Fold the paper in half without including a concertina fold.

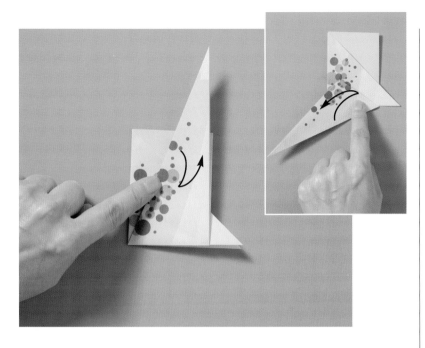

8 Turn back the long tip over the horizontal edge then fold the end back at an angle, making a second crease from the point it crosses the horizontal edge.

9 Lift the paper and open it up before pushing the long tip back inside, reversing the creases so that it now sits at an angle.

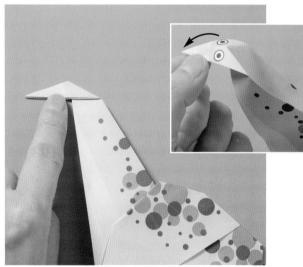

10 Slip the two parts of the model together, ensuring that they fit together snugly.

11 Turn over the top of the neck and make a crease. Open the neck and turn the point back around the outside, reversing the fold to form the head. Push the tip back inside to form a flat snout.

10 IGUANODON

The iguanodon was first discovered in 1825 by Gideon Mantell when he found a set of fossilized dinosaur teeth that looked similar to those of a modern day iguana. This model uses a two sheets of origami paper. Make sure the two parts join together cleanly by matching the folds and check that the feet are made with very crisp creases to make it stand up properly.

You will need:
Two sheets of 6 in (15 cm) square paper

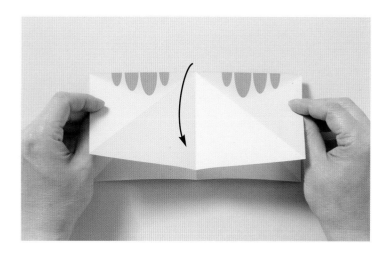

1 Fold the sheet of paper without the eyes from corner to corner both ways, opening out each time. Then fold it in half both ways, the second time through the middle of the design.

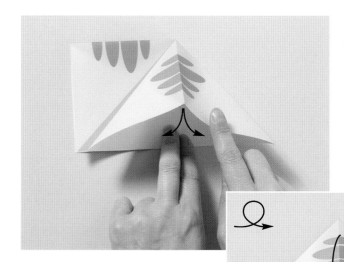

2 Lift the right-hand side of the paper to the vertical then press the top corner of the paper toward you, refolding the flap into a triangle. Turn over and repeat on the other side.

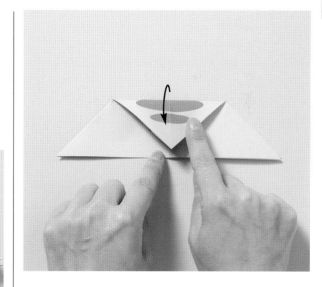

3 Fold the top of the triangle over so that the tip sits on the bottom edge of the paper.

4 Lift the upper edge of the paper and fold it back while holding the lower edge against the table. When the upper edge is also resting on the table press the inner sheets down to the sides to form triangles.

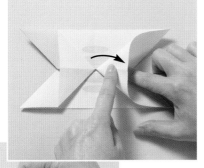

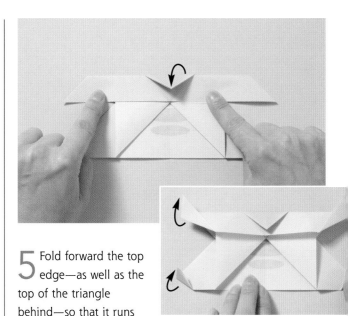

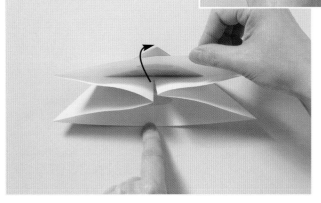

5 Fold forward the top edge—as well as the top of the triangle behind—so that it runs across the middle of the model. Fold over the four end points at the angles shown.

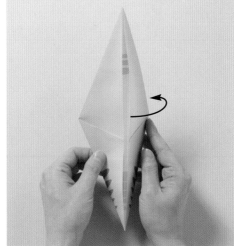

6 Take the second sheet of paper and fold it in half from corner to corner through the design and open. Fold the side points in so that the top edges now run down the center line then fold up the lower edges so they also run up the center line.

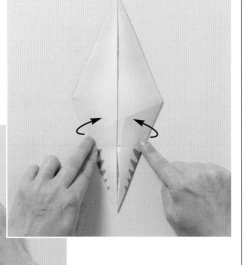

7 Lift the paper off the table and fold the model in half, pushing the right-hand side behind the left.

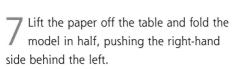

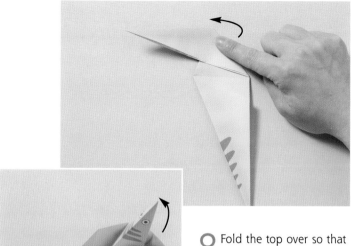

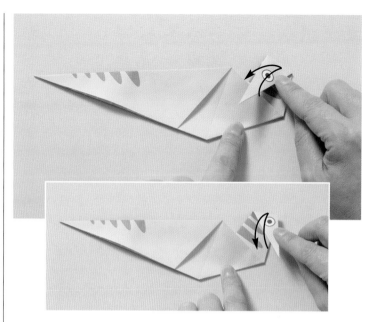

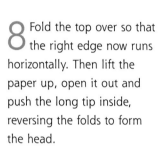

8 Fold the top over so that the right edge now runs horizontally. Then lift the paper up, open it out and push the long tip inside, reversing the folds to form the head.

9 Turn back the end of the head twice, first straight back down itself then at an angle downward.

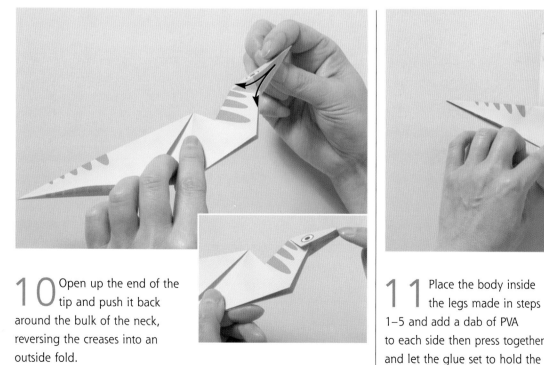

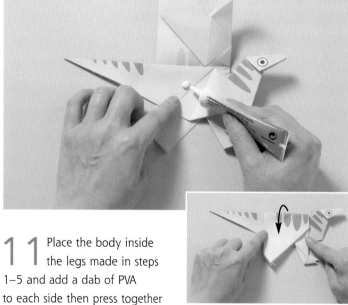

10 Open up the end of the tip and push it back around the bulk of the neck, reversing the creases into an outside fold.

11 Place the body inside the legs made in steps 1–5 and add a dab of PVA to each side then press together and let the glue set to hold the dinosaur together.

11 MEGALOSAURUS

The name megalosaurus is from the Greek meaning "Great Lizard". This is a genus of large meat-eating dinosaurs of the Middle Jurassic period that lived all across Europe. Take care through every step as you make this model because it is rather complex. If you find it tricky, practice first with as large a sheet of plain origami paper as you can find.

You will need:
One sheet of 6 in (15 cm) square paper

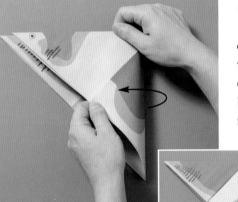

1 Fold the sheet in half both ways and from corner-to-corner both ways, the second time down the middle of the design. Fold in half again then lift the flap, open it out and refold as a diamond shape.

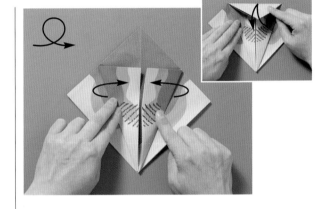

2 Turn the paper over and repeat, then fold the lower edges of the upper flaps in to meet each other along the center line. Fold down the top point to make a crease along the top of these flaps.

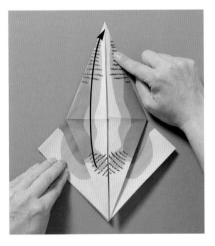

3 Open out the two top flaps and lift the bottom point, turning it back to form a long diamond shape in the center.

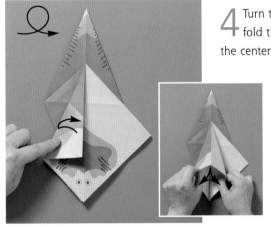

4 Turn the paper over and fold the left-hand point into the center so that the edge now runs down the center line. Immediately open out this fold, lift the flap and open it out, refolding it into a triangle.

5 Fold over the short, lower edges of the upper flap so that they meet along the center line.

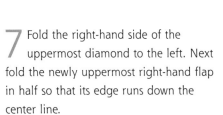

6 Open out the two flaps and lift the horizontal edge of paper, pushing it back so that the flap refolds into a diamond shape. Fold forward the small triangular top part of the diamond.

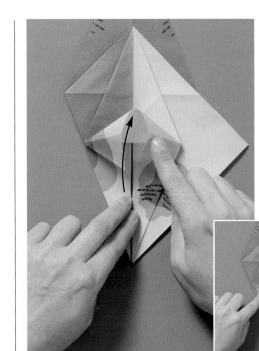

7 Fold the right-hand side of the uppermost diamond to the left. Next fold the newly uppermost right-hand flap in half so that its edge runs down the center line.

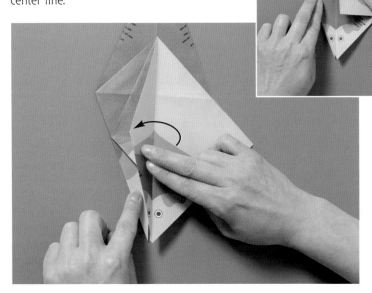

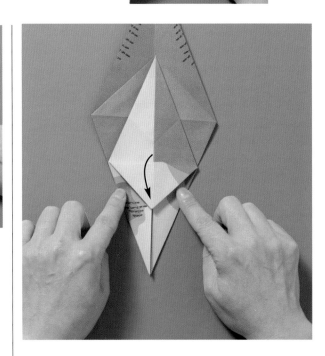

8 Now repeat the rest of steps 4, 5, and 6.

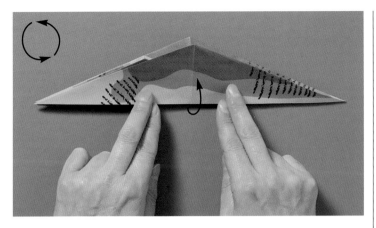

9 Turn the object through 90° then fold up the bottom half along the central crease.

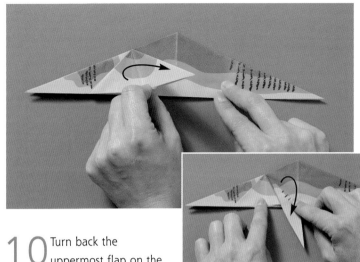

10 Turn back the uppermost flap on the left-hand end of the piece along the paper's length, then fold it down so the upper edge runs down the existing diagonal crease.

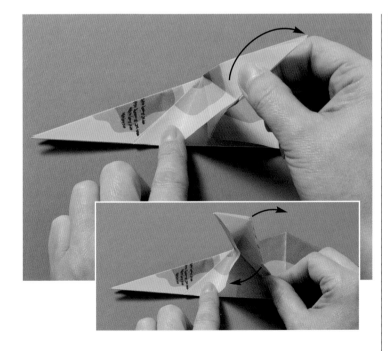

11 Keeping your left-hand finger in place, lift the flap and gently open it out, reversing the crease underneath the flap's right-hand side.

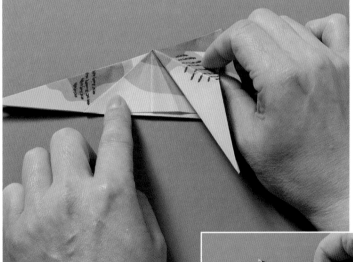

12 Refold the flap so that the paper that was behind it is now flat and there is a horizontal crease at its top. Next fold the flap along its length so that it points up to the left.

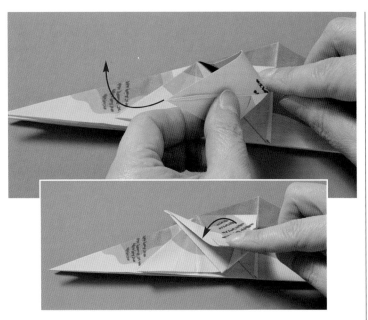

13 Lift and open the flap, reversing the direction of the inner crease, and fold the long tip back inside. Flatten the tip so that it again points up to the left.

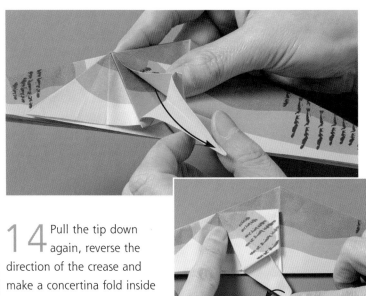

14 Pull the tip down again, reverse the direction of the crease and make a concertina fold inside so that the tip now points down to the right. Turn over the end to make the foot, before folding it in position inside the leg.

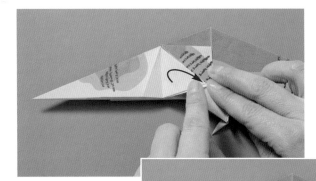

15 Turn the paper over and repeat steps 9–14 on the other side. When complete, turn over again and fold back the small triangle beside the leg and make a vertical crease across the long flap up from the bottom of the diagonal crease. Turn over and repeat on the other side.

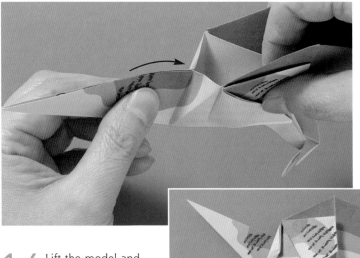

16 Lift the model and open it slightly then push the left-hand tips back into the body, reversing the creases. Flatten the dinosaur and fold forward half of the triangles folded back in the previous step.

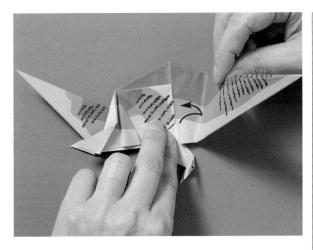

17 Make an angled crease across the right-hand tip from just above the backs of the dinosaur's legs.

18 Again lift the dinosaur and push in the right-hand tip, reversing the folds so that it now sits at an angle to the body.

19 Fold over the inner flaps on both sides so that the tail is held in position.

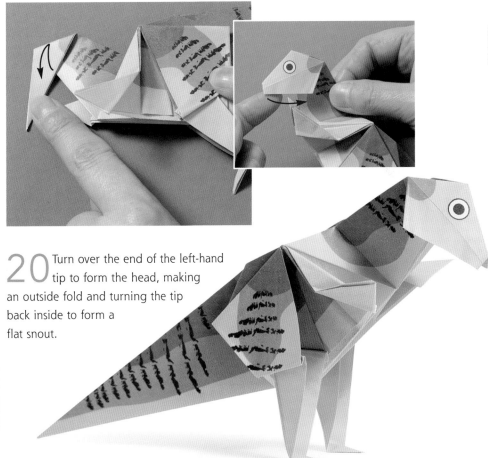

20 Turn over the end of the left-hand tip to form the head, making an outside fold and turning the tip back inside to form a flat snout.

12 PARASAUROLOPHUS

Parasaurolophus was a herbivore that walked both as a biped and a quadruped. It was part of a large family of dinosaurs that is best known for the extraordinary shapes of their skulls. The large crest sticking out the back of the head was probably used both to identify the different sexes and to help amplify their voice.

You will need:
Two sheets of 6 in (15 cm) square paper

1 Fold the sheet of paper without the eyes in half from corner to corner both ways, opening it out each time. Then fold it from side to side both ways. Turn the paper over and fold in the four corners to the center to make creases.

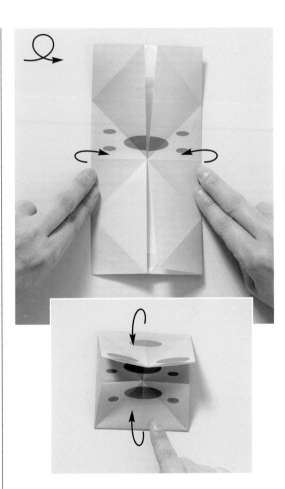

2 Turn the paper back over and fold the the sides into the center. Now fold the top and bottom in to meet in the center.

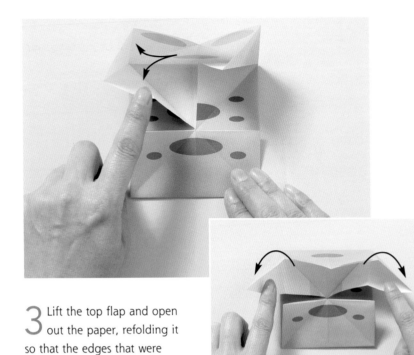

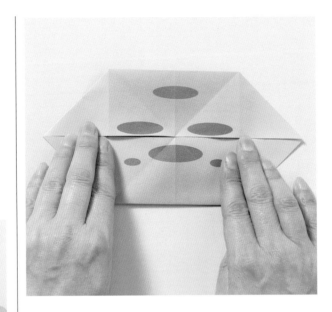

3 Lift the top flap and open out the paper, refolding it so that the edges that were running up the middle of the paper now run horizontally.

4 Repeat the refolding on the lower flap to make triangular shapes on both sides of the paper.

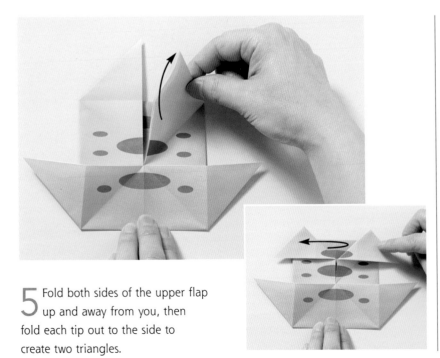

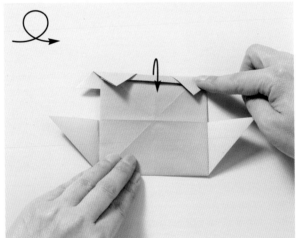

5 Fold both sides of the upper flap up and away from you, then fold each tip out to the side to create two triangles.

6 Turn the paper over and fold back the top edge, creating a new crease about ¼ in (0.5 cm) below the edge of the paper.

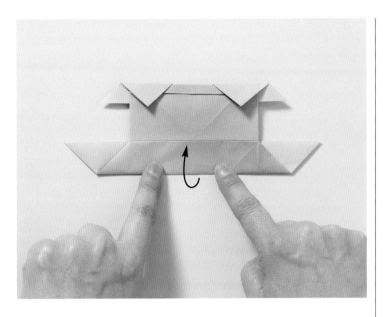

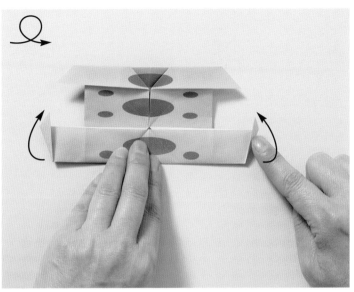

7 Fold up the bottom edge so that it runs across the middle of the paper.

8 Turn the paper back over and fold up the bottom corners at a slight angle to create the dinosaur's feet.

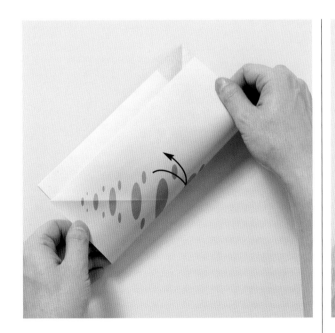

9 Take the second sheet of paper and fold it once from corner to corner up the middle of the design to make a crease, then open it out and fold from side to side to make a second crease line.

10 Fold over the left-hand corner until it sits on the second crease line and make a fold line to the top point. Fold in the left-hand edge so that the two edges run together.

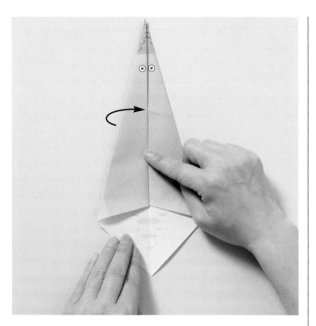

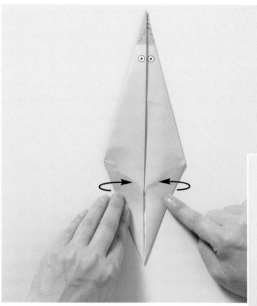

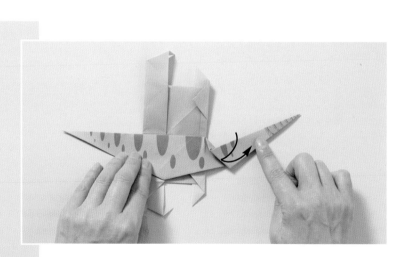

11 Turn over the left-hand side of the paper so that the edge runs down the central crease.

12 Fold the two short edges up to meet along the central line, then turn the right-hand side over along the central crease.

13 Spin the paper through 90° and position the body over the first sheet. Fold the right-hand tip down so that it runs vertically along the side of the second sheet then make a second angled fold about ½ in (1 cm) up.

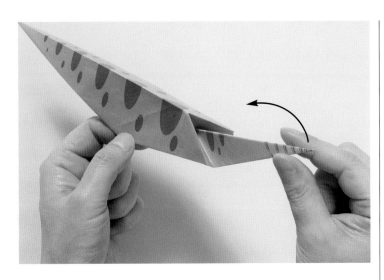

14 Lift up the body and open it slightly then push the tip back, making a concertina fold that leaves the tip sticking up at an angle.

15 turn over the right-hand tip to make an angled crease then open up the paper and reverse the crease creating an inside fold.

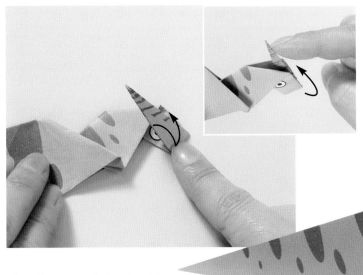

16 Turn back the tip with a right-angled crease then fold it inside the head to create the dinosaur's horn.

13 STEGOSAURUS

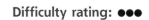
Stegosaurus means "covered lizard," from the large plates that stick up from the dinosaur's back that helped with self-defense and regulating the animal's temperature. This origami model is quite a challenge—the most complex part is making the back plates—so follow the descriptions closely and fold the creases tightly.

You will need:
One sheet of 12 in (30 cm) square paper

1 With the design upwards fold from corner to corner both ways, then open out and turn over before folding all four corners in to meet at the middle.

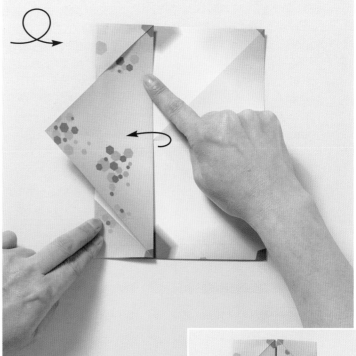

2 Turn the paper over and fold in both sides so that the edges meet down the center, letting the triangular tip stick out. Fold up the bottom and top to meet in the middle to make horizontal creases.

60

BIG DINOSAURS

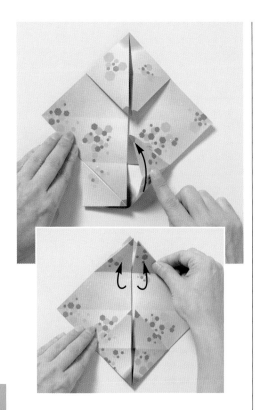

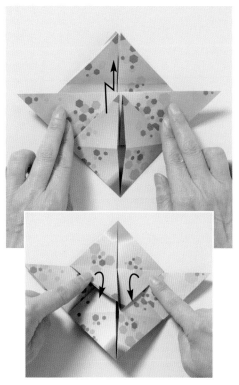

3 Open out the top and bottom and fold up the corner to the middle line, opening out the flaps and refolding them into a triangle. Turn back the bottom tips of the triangles at the top.

4 Make a concertina fold so that the widest horizontal crease now lies on the crease at the bottom of the top triangles. Fold the two triangular flaps at the top back over this edge.

5 Turn over the paper and release the flap of paper sitting behind the horizontal crease. Now fold the whole object in half.

6 Spin the paper through 90° and fold back the right-hand side of the left-hand triangle half so that its diagonal edge runs vertically. Release the right-hand triangle and fold its left-hand side in half too.

7 Lift the far left-hand point and, opening up the flap, push it upwards, refolding into a diamond shape.

8 Make two new creases by folding in the upper edges of the diamond so that they meet along the vertical crease.

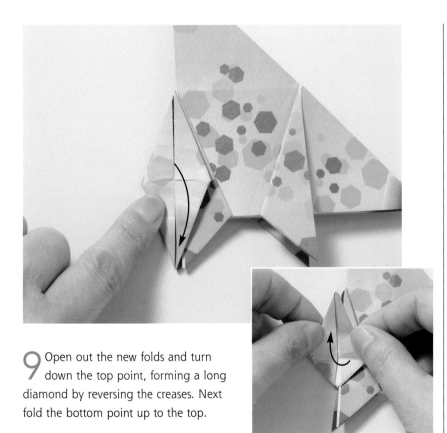

9 Open out the new folds and turn down the top point, forming a long diamond by reversing the creases. Next fold the bottom point up to the top.

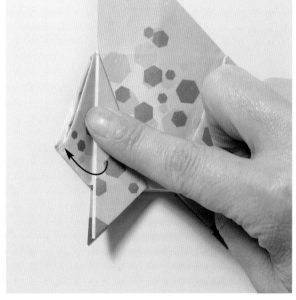

10 Fold the diamond in half by turning its right-hand side to the left.

STEGOSAURUS

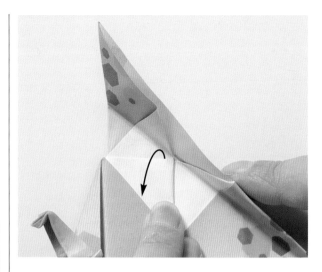

11 Pull forward the inner point and flatten it at an angle to form the dinosaur's neck. Now make a crease near the end and fold the tip inside the neck to form the head.

12 Carefully fold forward the uppermost flap that forms the body to reveal the reverse side of the lower flap. Gently make a crease from the right-hand corner through the middle of the square of visible blank paper.

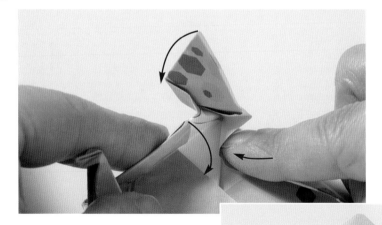

13 Keeping your right finger flat on the fold just made, turn over the other edge with your left hand and pull down the tip to form a diamond shape with its folds hidden underneath.

14 Now turn back the end of the diamond so that its edge is a continuation of the crease running down to the head.

15 Now turn the model over and repeat steps 12–14, making sure that the tip of the diamond ends up pointing forwards.

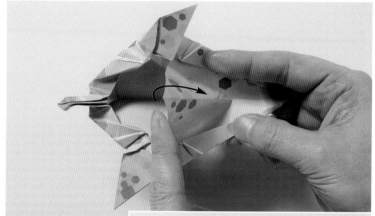

16 Open up the model and carefully pull back the uppermost inner flap, refolding it so that when the model is once again flat it sticks out of the back.

17 Open up the model again, this time pulling forward the remaining flap of paper and refolding it so that it sits between the dinosaur's head and the top spike.

14 SUPERSAURUS

The supersaurus is thought to be the biggest dinosaur of the long-necked, plant-eating diplodocus family. The model shown here was made with origami paper larger than the accompanying paper. If it seems tricky to make, practice first with a large square piece of thin wrapping paper, folding all the creases as flat as possible.

You will need:
One sheet of 6 in (15 cm) square paper

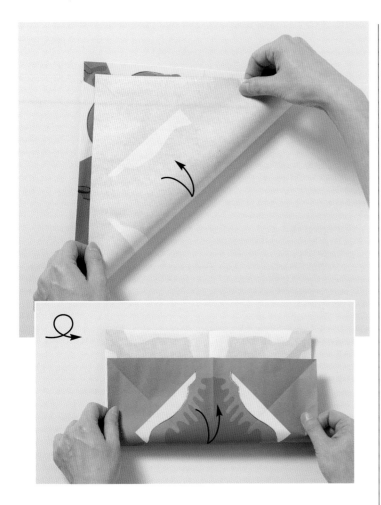

1 With the paper design side up fold in half both ways from corner to corner then turn over and fold it in half both ways.

2 Fold the bottom two corners in at an angle to meet on the center line then turn the paper over and fold forward the top two corners.

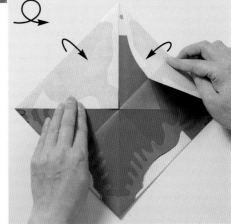

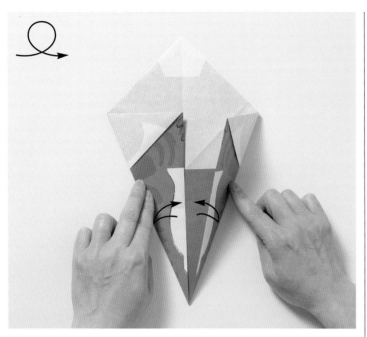

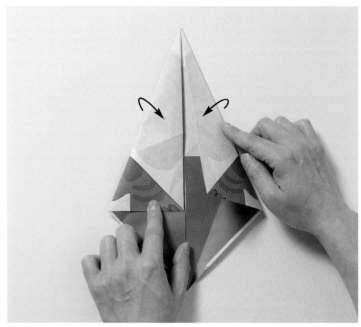

3 Turn the paper back over and make two creases by folding in the lower two sides so that they align along the center line. Then open them out.

4 Now fold in the upper two edges so that they meet along the center line and press them flat.

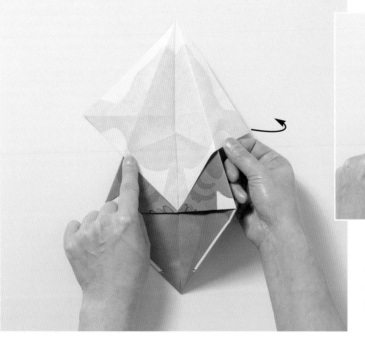

5 Unfold the loose flaps from behind the paper to create a diamond shape at the top of the model, then fold up the bottom of the paper to make a horizontal crease.

6 Lift each part of the bottom of the diamond and fold it up the center line, reversing the folds behind so that they flatten into triangular shapes.

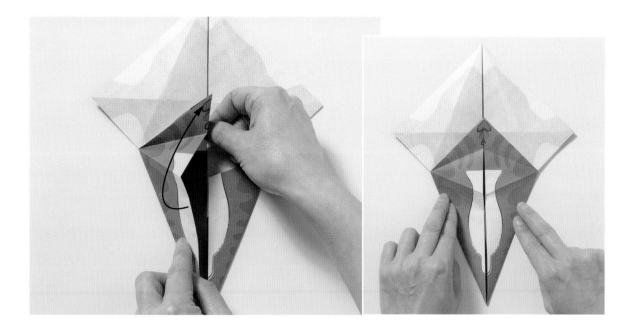

7 Fold back the upper parts of these triangles to reveal the diamond once again.

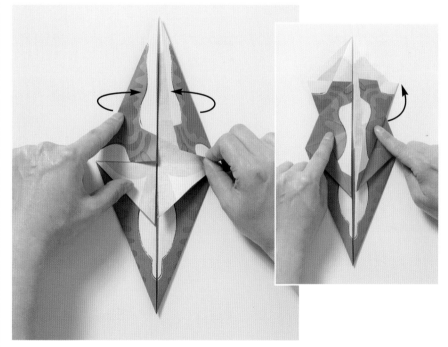

8 Fold over the upper edges of the diamond so that they meet along the center line. Then lift up the bottoms of these edges and turn them up the center line to make triangles pointig down the model.

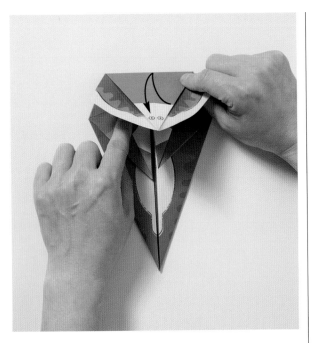

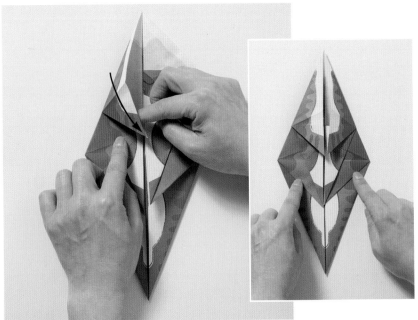

9 Fold the top of the object forward to make a crease.

10 Lift the horizontal edge of the upper triangles and turn them down the center line, reversing the creases.

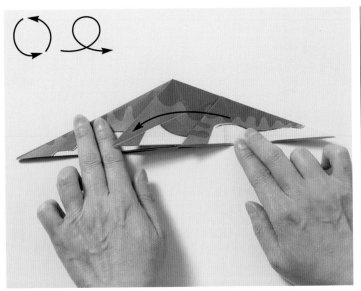

11 turn the object clockwise 90°, turn it over and fold it in half, turning the bottom up to the top.

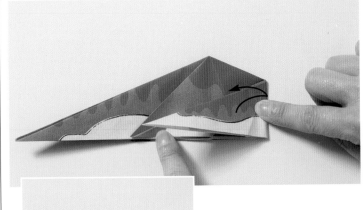

12 Make a crease across the right-hand end by turning the tip back along the horizontal line then release it and make a second angled crease to its right.

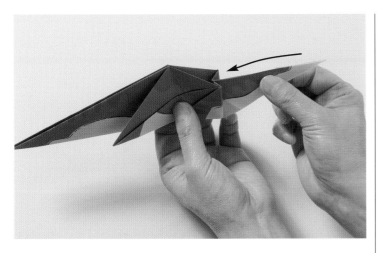

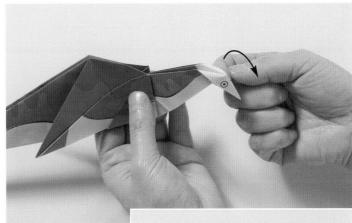

13 Lift up the object and, opening it slightly, push the tip back inside the body of the dinosaur, reversing the creases so that the tip sticks up at an angle.

14 Make an angled crease near the tip and then reverse the fold, turning the end around the outside. Turn up the point inside to create a flat snout.

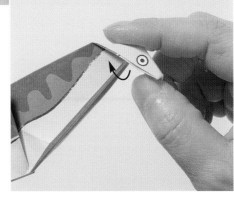

15 To finish, create the legs by folding the triangles along the dinosaur's body in half, making the left-hand edges run vertically. Turn over the model and repeat on the other side.

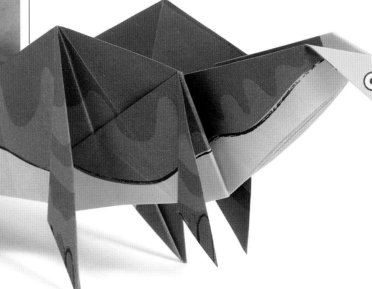

15 TYRANNOSAURUS REX

Tyrannosaurus Rex is by far the most popular and famous of all the dinosaurs. It was strong and ferocious, feared by every other dinosaur, but I have made a charming T. Rex that looks like it wouldn't hurt a fly. The model is relatively easy to make from two sheets of paper. The trick to making it beautiful is to fold a firm crease at its foot so it stands up well.

You will need:
Two sheets of 6 in (15 cm) square paper

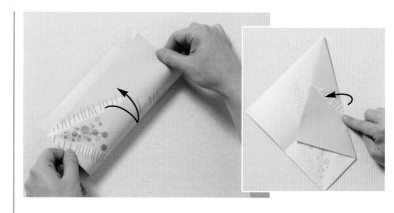

1 Fold the paper with the eyes from corner to corner down the middle of the design then open out and fold from side to side. Open again and fold the right-hand point across to the second crease line, making a new crease straight up to the top point.

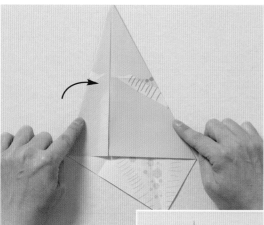

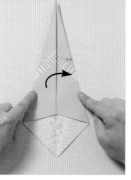

2 Fold over the left-hand side so that the two edges align then fold the left-hand side over again, using the line where the two edges meet as the fold line.

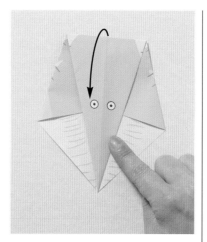

3 Fold the top point down so that it sits on top of the bottom point, making a horizontal fold.

4 Fold the top flap up to the right so that the left-hand edge runs across the top of the piece, then turn the point down so that the top edge now runs down the central crease.

BIG DINOSAURS

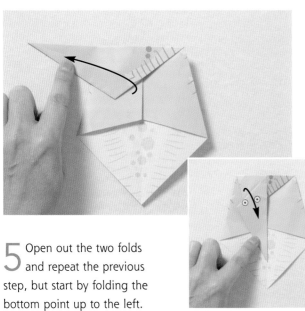

5 Open out the two folds and repeat the previous step, but start by folding the bottom point up to the left.

6 Open up the top flap then fold the short diagonal edges in to meet along the central crease. Lift the right-hand flap, open it up and reverse the diagonal crease, pushing the fold of paper underneath the top flap.

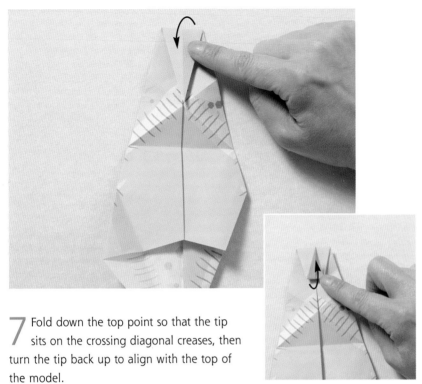

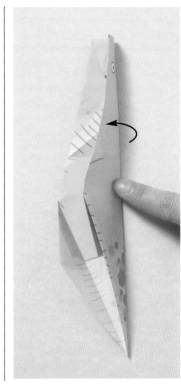

7 Fold down the top point so that the tip sits on the crossing diagonal creases, then turn the tip back up to align with the top of the model.

8 Fold the model in half along its central crease.

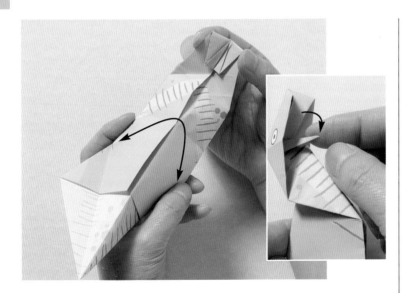

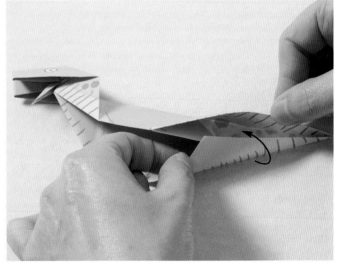

9 Lift up the model and open it out, then reverse the diagonal creases at the right-hand end and carefully refold to create an angled neck. Pull down the end point and flatten at an angle to create the T. Rex's mouth.

10 Fold the loose paper at the other end inside the opposite flap to hold the body together.

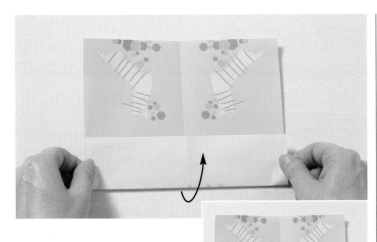

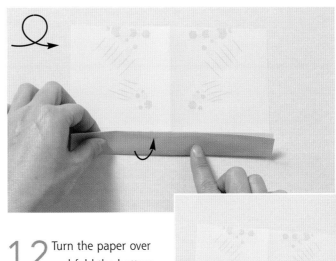

11 Take the second sheet of paper and fold it in half both ways then open it out and fold the bottom up to the central crease. Fold this flap in half by turning it back down to the bottom crease.

12 Turn the paper over and fold the bottom back up to the central crease, then fold the upper flap at the bottom of the paper over the central crease.

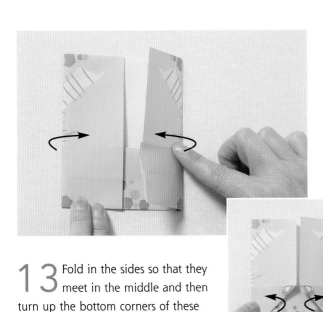

13 Fold in the sides so that they meet in the middle and then turn up the bottom corners of these new flaps, making diagonal creases with the bottom edges now running up the sides of the model.

14 Lift the main flap on each side opening out the smaller triangular flaps. Then refold the main flaps, reversing the diagonal creases so the smaller flaps now point out over the sides of the model.

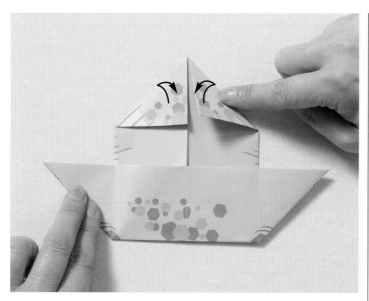

15 Fold down the top two corners so that the top edges now align down the center of the model to make two diagonal creases.

16 Lift the top corners of the model and push them inside, reversing the direction of the creases and refold so that the top of the model is now a single, central point.

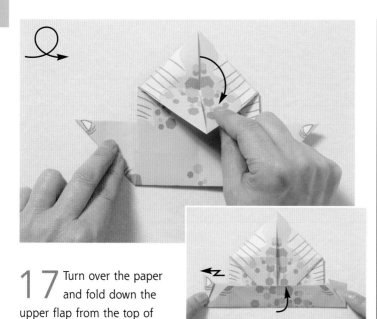

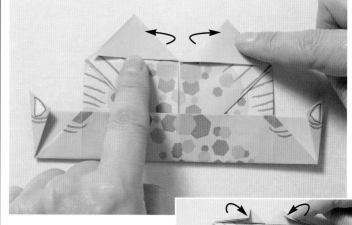

17 Turn over the paper and fold down the upper flap from the top of the model. Next turn up the bottom edge so that it runs along the widest horizontal edge. Turn over the outside points using concertina folds.

18 Fold over the two flaps at the top of the model so that the vertical edges run horizontally. Fold over the outside diagonal edges of these new triangles so that they also run horizontally.

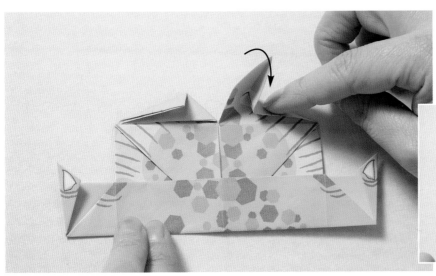

19 Lift the last flaps and open them out, then refold into the same shape while reversing the direction of the creases so that the flaps are on the outside. Turn these flaps up to the vertical.

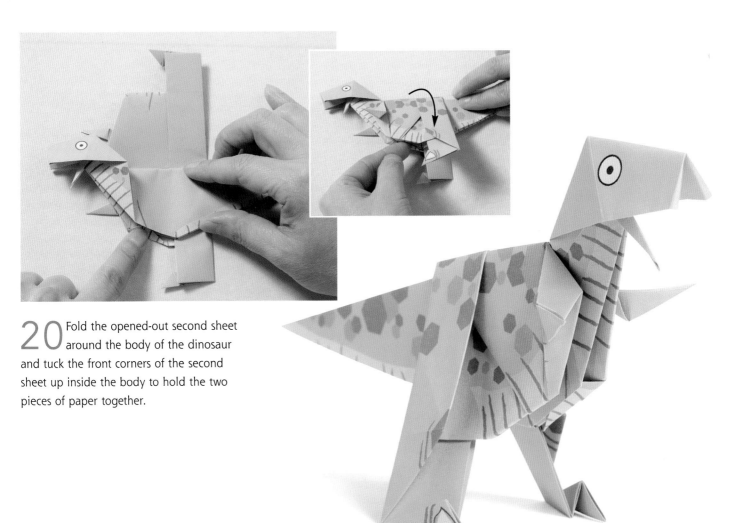

20 Fold the opened-out second sheet around the body of the dinosaur and tuck the front corners of the second sheet up inside the body to hold the two pieces of paper together.

16 **TRICERATOPS**

Difficulty rating: ●●●

Triceratops usually had a docile nature but—as its name, meaning "face with three horns," suggests—it was happy to use its size and fight off predators if it was needed. Although it looks complicated, this adorable triceratops is easy to make once you have become accustomed to connecting the body with the head.

You will need:
Two sheets of 6 in (15 cm) square paper

1 Take the sheet with the eyes and fold it in half both ways to make creases. Then fold up the bottom to the central creases and the sides in so that they meet in the middle.

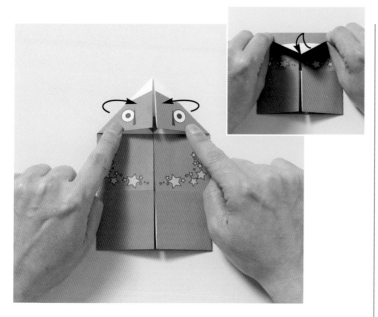

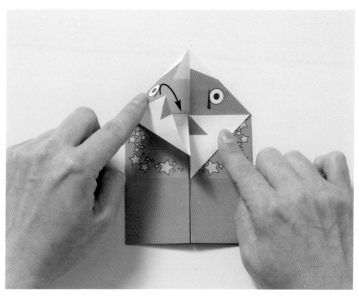

2 Turn down the top two corners so that they meet on the center line and then turn the top over to make a crease along the bottom of these new flaps.

3 Lift up each of the triangular flaps and pull out the inside corners from the top, reversing the creases and folding them down the middle of the model.

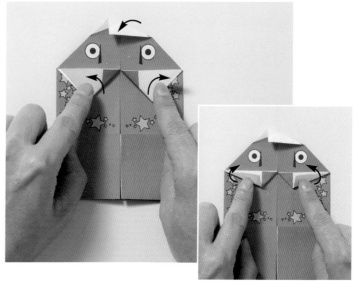

4 Turn over the top point so that it sits on the line between the bases of the diagonal edges, making a crease along the upper edge. Lift the flap and fold both its edges in turn so that they run along the crease line just made.

5 Fold the bottom points made in step 3 up and across to the outside of the model so that the vertical edges now run horizontally. Turn up the bottom points on each side so that the outer diagonal edges also run horizontally.

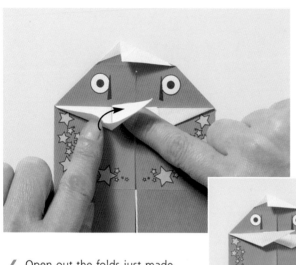

6 Open out the folds just made and pull out the inner flaps, while keeping a finger on the inside. Refold the flap, reversing the inner creases to make a long point across the model, with a new vertical crease inside. Turn up the bottoms of the main flaps so that the vertical edges now run horizontally.

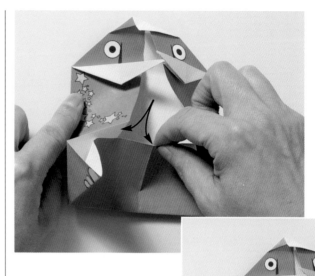

7 Open out the new triangles and fold over the inside to the outside to form triangles.

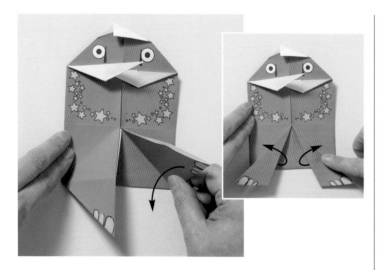

8 Turn down these triangles so that the horizontal edges now run vertically, before folding these edges over so that they run down the existing diagonal creases.

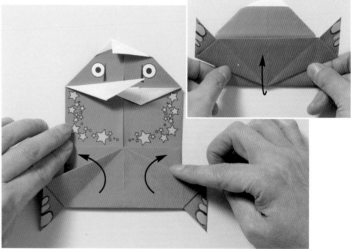

9 Fold these flaps upward along the diagonal creases and then turn up the bottom of the object across the horizontal edges.

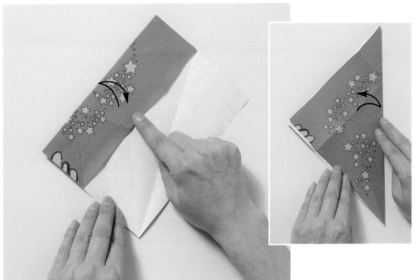

10 Take the second sheet of paper and fold it from corner to corner both ways, then fold in both sides so that the lower diagonal edges run up the center of the paper.

11 Open up the paper again and make new creases by folding over the upper edges so that the corners align with the tops of the creases just made. Open out once more and fold in half.

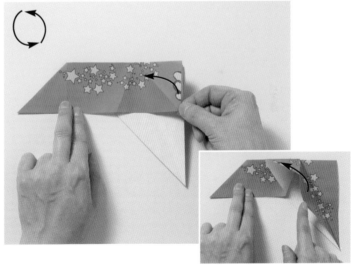

12 Lift up the paper and fold in half again, this time reversing the main length of the central crease so that the edges fold around it, leaving a point at the top of the object.

13 Spin the paper through 90° then lift the lower, right-hand corner of the flap and turn it over to the left-hand end of the top edge, making a new diagonal crease from the bottom point. Turn the paper over and repeat on the other side.

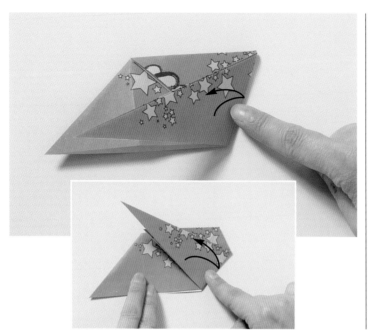

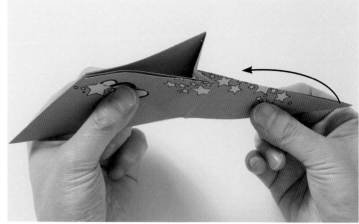

15 Now make a concertina fold from these two creases by pushing the long point inside the object to make an angled tail.

14 Turn the paper back and fold over the bottom right-hand point so that it sits on the left-hand point. Open it up again and refold it so that its lower edge lies on top of itself.

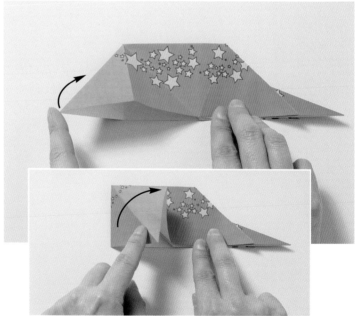

16 Fold forward the triangular flaps on both sides of the model.

17 Push over the left-hand point of the model and open up the piece so that it refolds into a square flap with the point still sitting on the bottom edge of the paper.

18 Fold back the triangular flap so that the diagonal edge now runs down the vertical edge of the square flap. Turn over and repeat, then turn the model back and fold the bottom right corner of the square flap up to the top left corner.

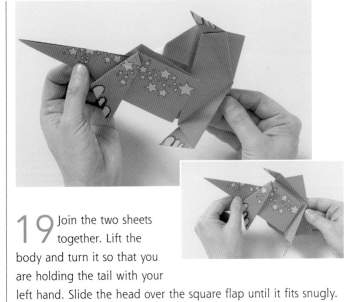

19 Join the two sheets together. Lift the body and turn it so that you are holding the tail with your left hand. Slide the head over the square flap until it fits snugly.

20 Keeping hold with your left hand, turn the head towards you until it is at right angles to the body.

21 Press the two sides of the head together. As you do this it will tilt upward until it creates new diagonal creases on which it sits soundly.

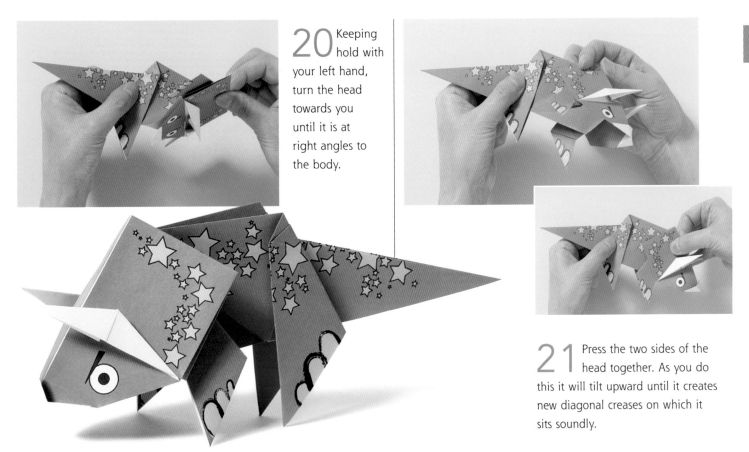

DINOSAURS sky

17 CAUDIPTERYX

Caudipteryx lived about 140 million years ago, just as the first birds were beginning to evolve. It was a powerful and agile hunter with a very short tail, long clawed feet and small, wing-like limbs. However caudipteryx was unable to fly—making it an intermediate species between land-bound dinosaurs and the first flying birds.

You will need:
One sheet of 6 in (15 cm) square paper
Scissors

1 Fold the paper in half from corner to corner, open and repeat in the other direction. Fold the four corners in so that they meet at the center point.

2 Fold over the two left-hand corners so that they too meet in the middle, making a point for the beak. Fold over the top half of the paper along the center line.

3 Turn over the left-hand end of the model at an angle to make a crease. Then open up that end of the model and fold the tip inside, reversing the diagonal crease.

4 Lift up the paper and fold back the flap on the right-hand side. Now cut about two-thirds of the way along the diagonal edge with a pair of scissors, up to the point where the design is showing through the paper.

5 Turn the right-hand flap back in and fold the model in half again. Fold up the bottom edge at a slight angle to make the wing. Turn over and repeat on the other side.

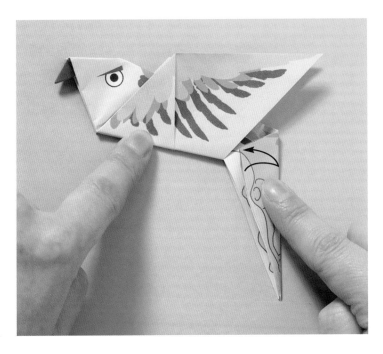

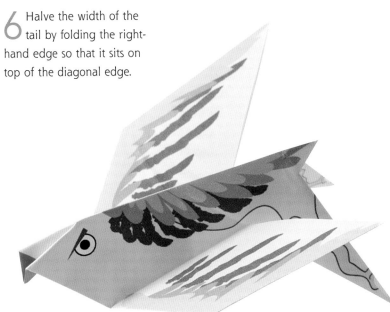

6 Halve the width of the tail by folding the right-hand edge so that it sits on top of the diagonal edge.

7 Open out the crease and make a short angled cut down the back edge of the design to the crease. Then cut along the top crease to join.

8 Open up the model and fold the tail back on itself along the diagonal creases, then fold the paper up again to finish.

18 ICARONYCTERIS

Difficulty rating: ●○○

Icaronycteris is a very early, extinct member of the bat family that lived just after the last of the dinosaurs died out approximately 50 million years ago. They flew from tree to tree taking their prey, just like modern bats. This model is very easy to make but young children should always ask an adult for help when using scissors.

You will need:
One sheet of 6 in (15 cm) square paper
Scissors

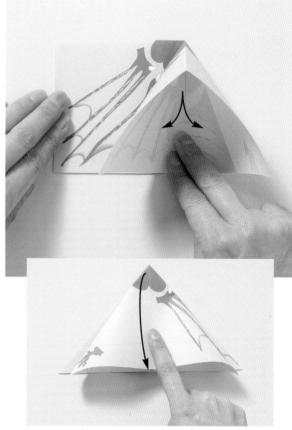

1 With the sheet of paper design side down, fold in half, open, and repeat in the other direction. Lift the right-hand side, open out the flap and refold as a triangle. Turn over and repeat.

2 Turn back over and cut a curve around the design at the top from the right-hand side to a point about ¼ in (0.5 cm) from the central crease.

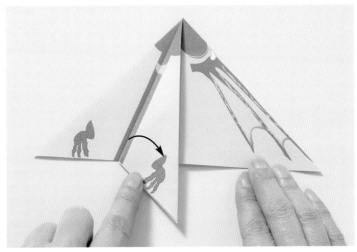

3 Fold over the top flap on the left-hand side of the piece so that the edge now runs down the central crease.

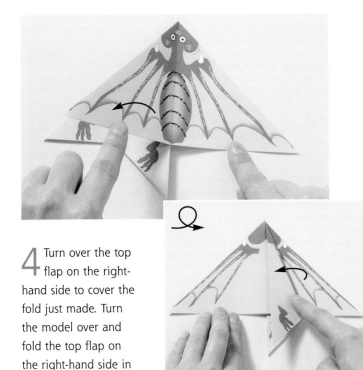

4 Turn over the top flap on the right-hand side to cover the fold just made. Turn the model over and fold the top flap on the right-hand side in half to match that made in step 3.

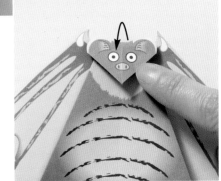

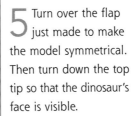

5 Turn over the flap just made to make the model symmetrical. Then turn down the top tip so that the dinosaur's face is visible.

19 TUPUXUARA

Flying through the trees of the prehistoric jungle the mighty tupuxuara hunted from the air, seeking out its prey on the ground below. Make your origami model and hang it from the ceiling or, even better, let it fly across the room like the earliest ancestors of the birds.

You will need:
One sheet of A5 (8¼ x 6 in/21 x 15 cm) paper

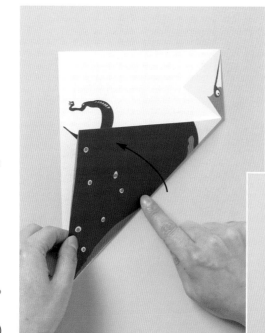

1 With the colored side down, fold the paper in half then fold the bottom, creased corner across to the left-hand edge. Fold down the top right-hand corner so that the edges of the two flaps run together and open out.

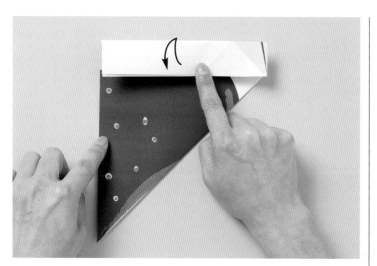

2 Turn down the top edge, using the flap as the fold line, and make a crease. Then open out again and fold the top down so that this time it runs along the edge of the flap and make another crease.

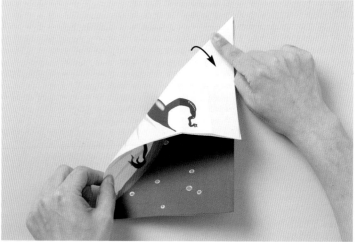

3 Open out the diagonal folds and then turn the top across so that it aligns with the left-hand side of the piece and make a firm fold from the top corner, but only as far as the first crease line.

SKY DINOSAURS

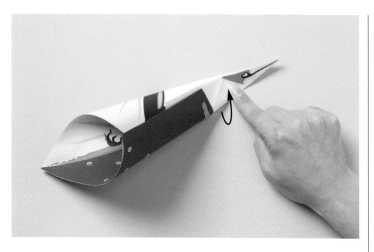

4 Turn over the whole left-hand side of the model and press down against the right-hand edge, again only making a crease as far as the first diagonal crease line.

5 Open out the whole sheet of paper and fold the left-hand edge down to the bottom to make a diagonal fold.

6 Lift the vertical edge where the design of the beak touches it and fold it down and to the left, making a new horizontal edge across the top of the object.

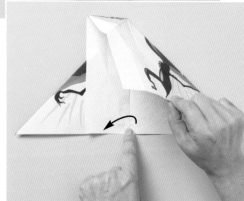

7 Let the flaps open slightly and fold the vertical edge to the left. Then turn the horizontal edge down to lie on top of it, creating a triangle shape with a flap sticking up.

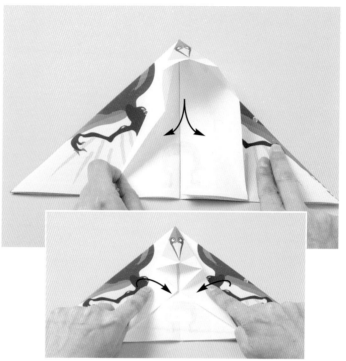

8 Fold down the two sides of the flap, flattening it and creating a triangle for the head. Fold in the sides of the head so that they meet along the model's center line.

9 Open out the flaps again, lift up the head and reverse the diagonal creases below, before pressing the head flat again.

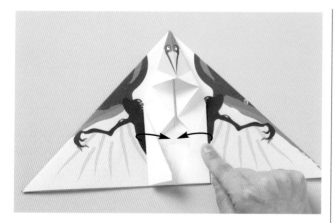

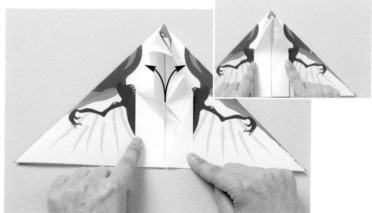

10 Fold in the bottom corners of the flap so that they meet on the center line, creating vertical creases up each side of the flap.

11 Open out one side of the pocket before refolding it so that its edge runs up the center line. Repeat on the other side, leaving the head lifted away from the table.

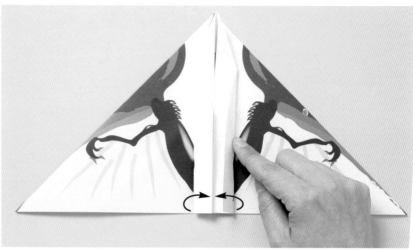

12 Carefully open up the head and reverse the three diagonal folds underneath, reforming the head to create the beak.

13 Fold in both edges of the pocket to meet along the center line

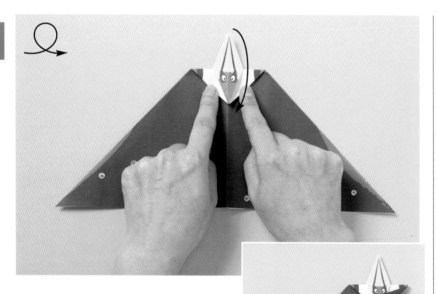

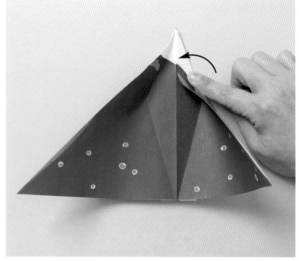

14 Turn over the model and fold down the head, allowing the beak to break out the top. Fold over the outer tips to form the wing creases, making fold lines from the middle at the bottom to the side of the head fold.

15 Open out the model and fold the edges into to the center but only making firm folds as far down as the diagonal crease.

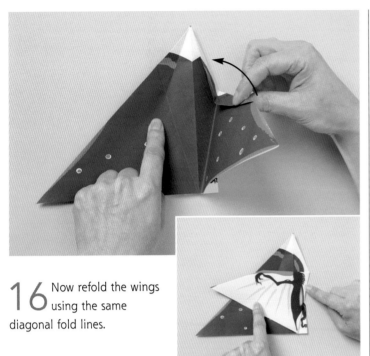

16 Now refold the wings using the same diagonal fold lines.

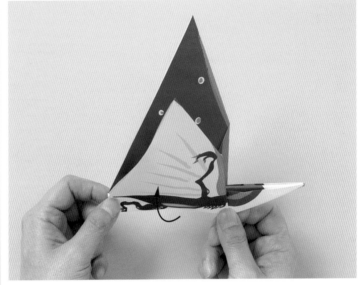

17 Lift up the model and fold it in half along its length.

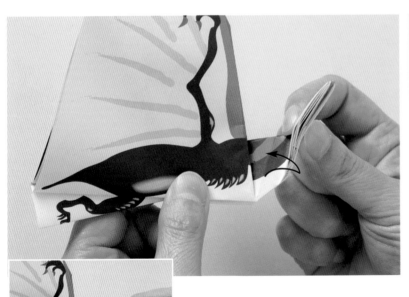

18 Make a diagonal crease in front of the wings then open up the flap, reverse the new fold, and push the head up to form the neck.

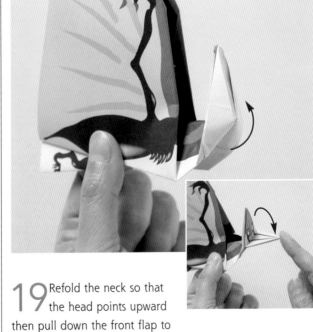

19 Refold the neck so that the head points upward then pull down the front flap to open up the face. Finally, fold down the wings parallel to the body.

20 PTERANODON

Pteranodon were massive flying reptiles—with wings up to 6 meters across—that lived near the coast, and probably fed off sea creatures such as fish and squid. This model has been created using three sheets of paper to represent the huge wings. When you make the second wing, remember to reverse all the folds so that they are mirror images of each other.

You will need:
Three sheets of 6 in (15 cm) square paper
Paper glue

1 Color side up, fold the paper with the eyes in half both ways. Then turn it over and fold it in half from corner to corner both ways, the second time down the middle of the design.

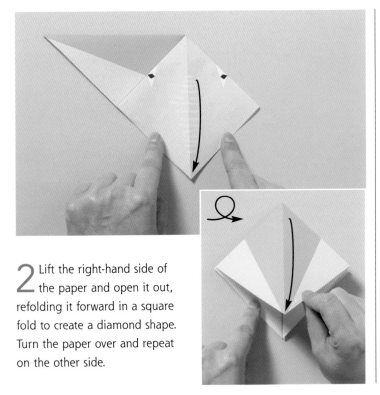

2 Lift the right-hand side of the paper and open it out, refolding it forward in a square fold to create a diamond shape. Turn the paper over and repeat on the other side.

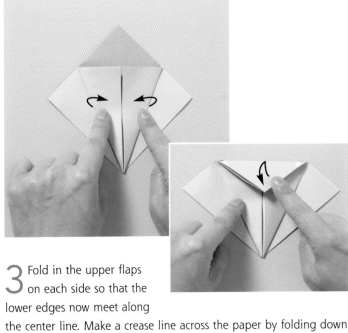

3 Fold in the upper flaps on each side so that the lower edges now meet along the center line. Make a crease line across the paper by folding down the top point over the new creases.

99

PTERANODON

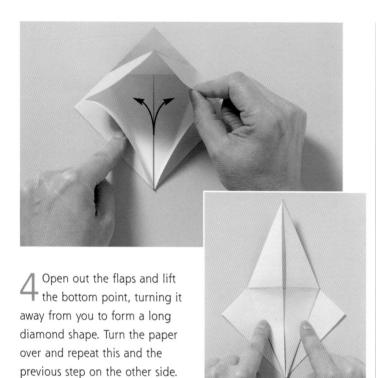

4 Open out the flaps and lift the bottom point, turning it away from you to form a long diamond shape. Turn the paper over and repeat this and the previous step on the other side.

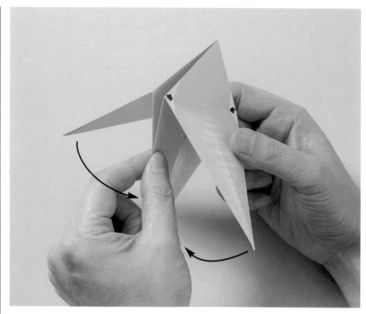

5 Lift the model off the table and fold down the two upper points so that they sit with the lower point.

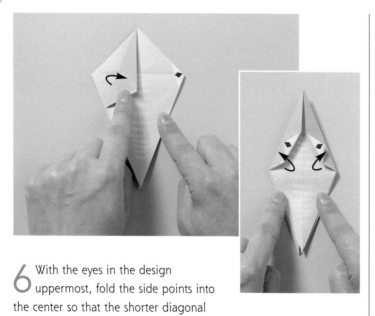

6 With the eyes in the design uppermost, fold the side points into the center so that the shorter diagonal edges now run down the central crease. Turn the paper over and repeat. Turn the paper back over and fold back the corners of the flaps to reveal the eyes.

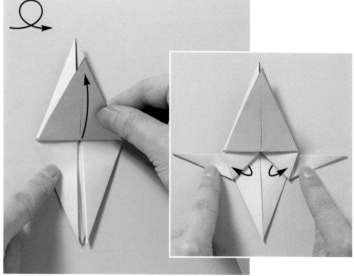

7 Turn the paper over again and fold up the flap from the bottom. Next turn the two points to the sides, folding them underneath themselves.

8 Fold the model in half along its center line. Then lift it off the table and gently prise down the inner flap from the top, refolding this at an angle to form the mouth.

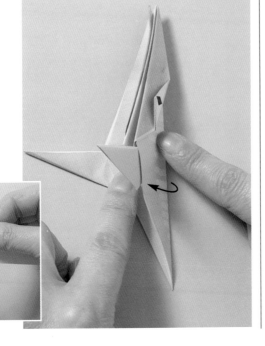

9 Take the sheet of paper from which you will create the right wing and fold it in half from corner to corner as shown. Then fold up the top sheet so that the left hand edge now runs across the horizontal edge.

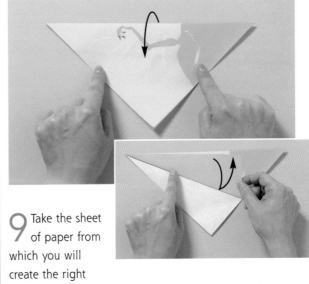

10 Open out the fold and turn over the upper sheet so that the lower end of the right-hand edge runs along the crease. Open out again and fold both sheets up to run along the new crease.

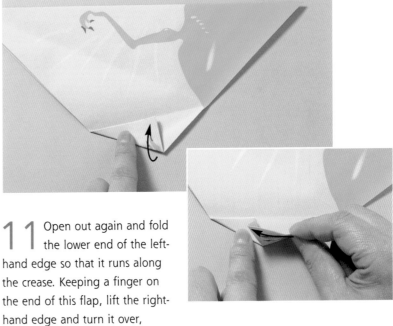

11 Open out again and fold the lower end of the left-hand edge so that it runs along the crease. Keeping a finger on the end of this flap, lift the right-hand edge and turn it over, refolding what was the bottom point long the edge of the fold.

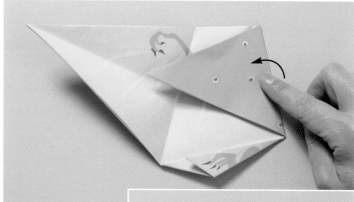

12 Turn over the left-hand point of the model so that its diagonal edge now aligns with the flap made in the previous step.

13 Open out the last fold and turn over the right-hand point so that its diagonal edge runs down the central crease. Next turn back the tip of this flap ensuring that the folded edge sits on top of itself.

14 Lift the last flap up and open it out, refolding it with a square fold into a diamond shape. Then turn back the loose point, making a fold across the widest point.

15 Fold in the bottom edges of the diamond shape made in the last step.

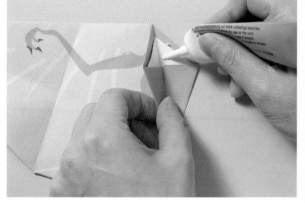

16 Use paper glue to stick the two sides of the diamond together.

17 Put the wing to one side and take the final sheet of paper, repeating steps 9–16 in reverse to form the left-hand wing.

18 Place the two wings on the table and use the glue to fix them together, sticking the two triangles of paper to each other.

19 Carefully insert the two spikes at the bottom of the head into the pockets of the wing flaps, pushing the head in as far as possible to create a tight fit.

marine
DINOSAURS

21 DUNKLEOSTEUS

Living about 380 million years ago, long before the dinosaurs even existed, dunkleosteus was one of the largest fish that has ever lived—reaching up to 10 meters long. Looking like a violent brute, it was powerfully built with strong armor-plating round its head, but even so was streamlined and shark-like. This model is very simple—everyone will have fun making it!

You will need:
One sheet of 6 in (15 cm) square paper

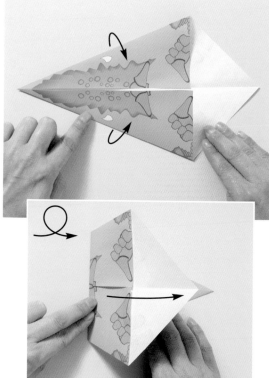

1 With the paper design-side down, make a crease from corner to corner down the length of the design. Then open it out and fold the right-hand edges in so that they meet along the central crease. Turn the object over and fold it in half.

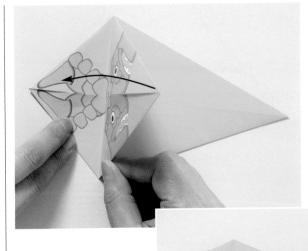

2 Lift the corners of the upper flaps and turn them to the left, refolding the flaps into long points.

3 Turn the upper flap from the right-hand side to the left and then turn back the point so that it sits on the vertical crease.

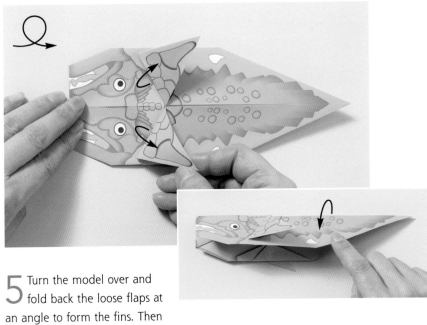

4 Turn the top and bottom points into the middle, making horizontal creases.

5 Turn the model over and fold back the loose flaps at an angle to form the fins. Then fold the model in half along its length.

22 FUTABASAURUS

Futabasaurus was a giant swimming plesiosaur that was recently discovered in eastern Japan by a young high-school student. Even though it was about 7 meters long many of the bones are damaged, which suggests that it was hunted by sharks. When you have made the model you can hang it from the ceiling so that it looks like it is swimming through the ancient ocean.

You will need:
Two sheets of 6 in (15 cm) square paper

MARINE DINOSAURS

1 Take the sheet of paper with the eyes and fold it in half from corner to corner down the length of the design. Then open it out and fold the bottom right-hand side up to make a second crease.

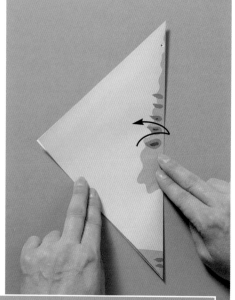

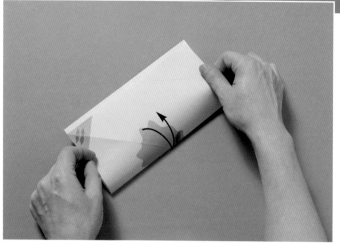

2 Fold in the right-hand point so that it sits on the diagonal crease, making a fold to the top point, then fold in the left-hand side so that the upper edge aligns with the first fold.

3 Turn over the top point so that it sits on the bottom point, then turn this tip back so that it is aligned with the diagonal edge of paper underneath.

4 Open out the entire sheet and fold down the top point so that it sits on the nearest horizontal crease.

5 Fold in the sides as before, so that the edges align, then fold over the left-hand edge again so that it runs down the paper's main vertical crease.

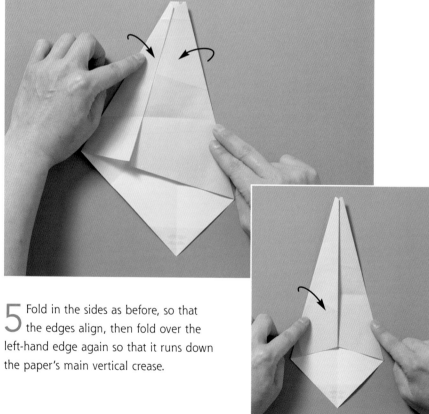

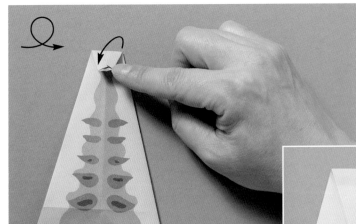

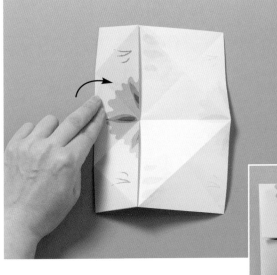

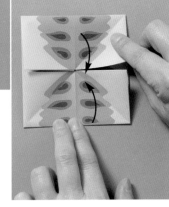

6 Turn the paper over and fold back the top point about ½ in (1 cm) down. Then fold the top down so that the corners of this new crease sit on the diagonal edges of the model.

7 Turn back the upper flap making a new crease, about ½ in (1 cm) from the original middle crease.

8 Take the second sheet of paper and, design side down, fold in half from corner to corner and side to side, opening up each fold. Turn the sheet over and fold all four corners in so that they meet in the center.

9 Open out the flaps and fold in the sides of the paper so that they align down the central crease. Then turn over the top and bottom so that they also meet in the middle.

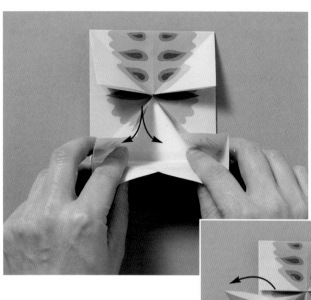

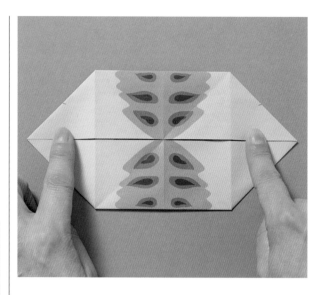

10 Lift the lower flap and open it out, refolding it so that the corners of the paper are turned to the outside, creating new triangular flaps.

11 Repeat with the upper flap so that the paper now forms a lozenge shape.

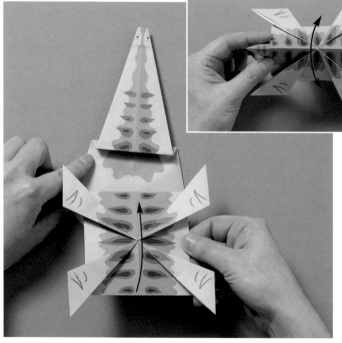

12 Fold over each of these corners so that the edges run along the diagonal creases.

13 Slide the second sheet into the concertina fold of the first sheet and then lift both away from the table and fold them in half along the model's length.

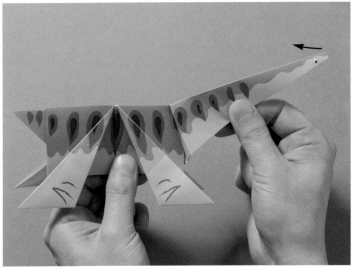

14 Open up the model again and turn over the loose flaps on each side to hold the two sheets of paper together.

15 Push the long tip up and refold it at an angle to create the neck.

16 Turn up the tip at an angle to make a crease, then refold it around the neck to form the head.

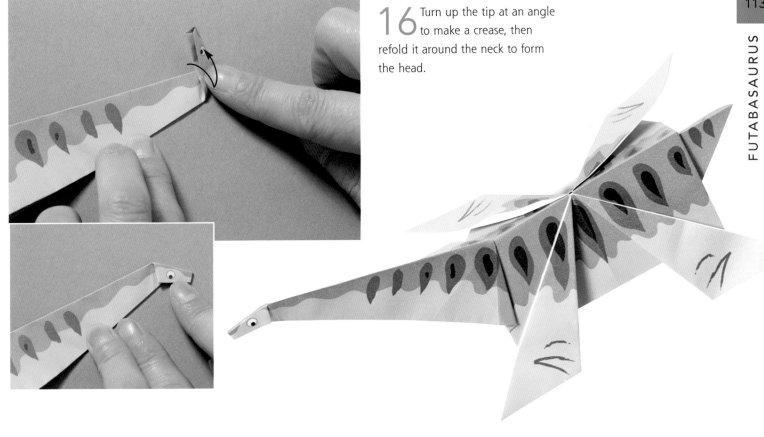

23 ICHTHYOSAURUS

Difficulty rating: ●○○

Ichthyosaurus was a small swimming dinosaur that lived in the seas around modern-day Europe. When it was found in the early 19th century by Mary Anning in England it was the first complete dinosaur fossil to be discovered. This model is made using the traditional Japanese origami fish as its base and should be very easy for anyone to make.

You will need:
One sheet of 6 in (15 cm) square paper

1 Fold the paper in half from corner to corner through the middle of the design to make a crease. Then open up again and fold in the two side points so that the lower edges of the sheet meet along the central crease.

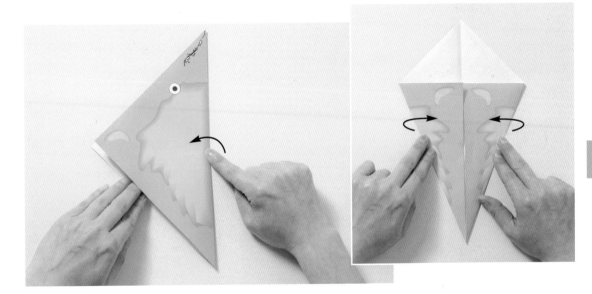

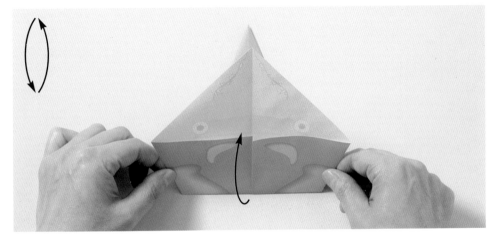

2 Turn the paper over and spin it round, then fold the bottom point up so that it sits on the top point.

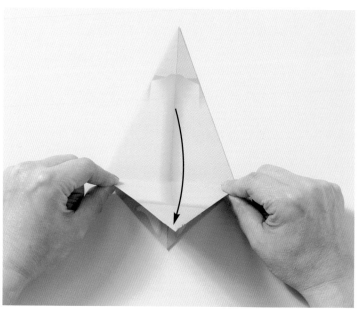

3 Lift the top flaps and fold them down, refolding the flaps so that the corners are at the bottom.

4 Fold down the upper flap from the top to make a long diamond shape.

5 Fold back the bottom point so that the tip sits on the horizontal crease, and make a new crease.

6 Fold down the same tip, making a new crease about ¼ in (0.5 cm) up from the original.

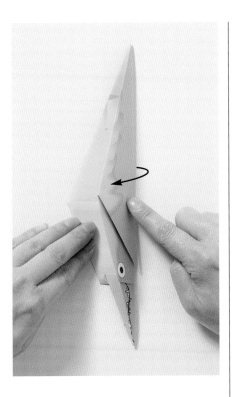

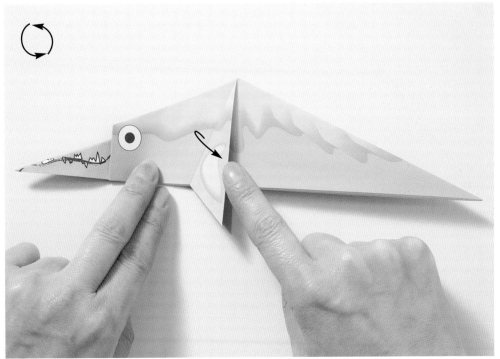

7 Fold the model in half along the main central crease.

8 Fold the top flaps in half to form the dinosaur's fins, making sure that the diagonal edge now runs vertically.

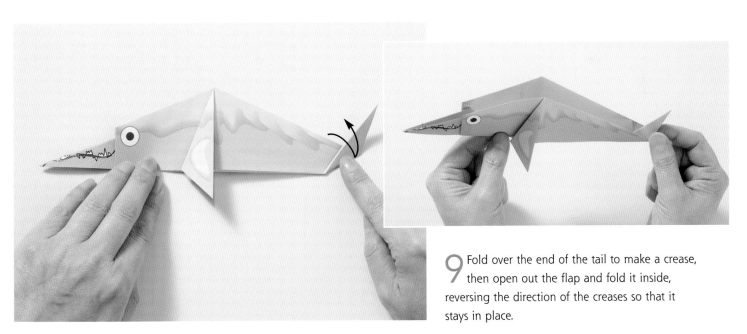

9 Fold over the end of the tail to make a crease, then open out the flap and fold it inside, reversing the direction of the creases so that it stays in place.

24 MOSASAURUS

The carnivorous mosasaurus was a marine dinosaur that lived during the late Cretaceous period about 65 million years ago. Its huge body of more than 10 meters was similar to modern-day crocodiles and it is thought that it swam across the ocean surface, hunting sea turtles and other marine reptiles as well as fish, squid, ammonites, and other shellfish.

You will need:
Two sheets of 6 in (15 cm) square paper

1 Fold the paper without eyes in half to make a crease and open out. Fold in the sides to meet along the central crease.

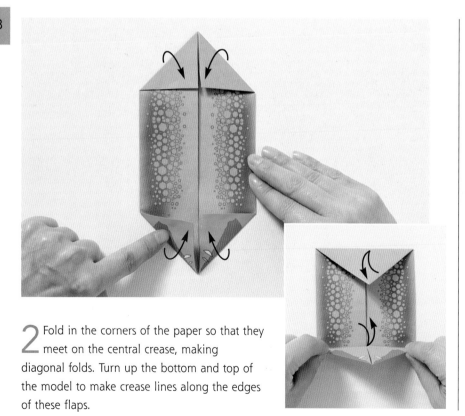

2 Fold in the corners of the paper so that they meet on the central crease, making diagonal folds. Turn up the bottom and top of the model to make crease lines along the edges of these flaps.

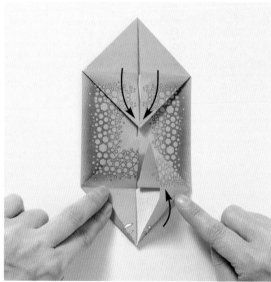

3 Open out the corner flaps and refold them, pushing the corners of the paper sitting on the central crease towards the middle of the model, and reforming the flaps into triangles.

MARINE DINOSAURS

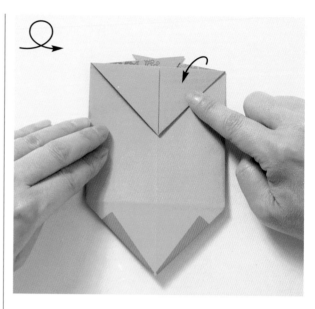

4 Fold the lower two flaps down so that all four flaps point downward, then fold each flap in half so that the diagonal edge runs across the horizontal crease.

5 Turn the model over and fold down the top point across the horizontal crease.

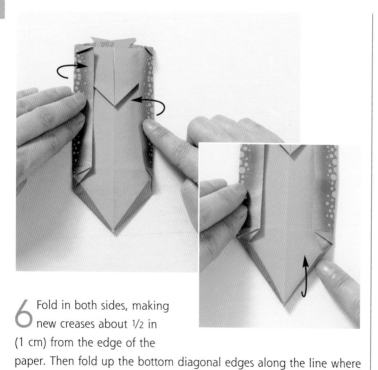

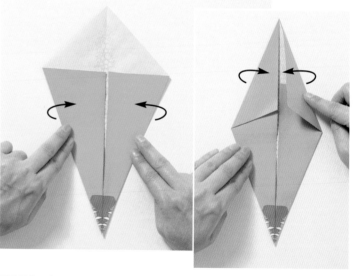

6 Fold in both sides, making new creases about ½ in (1 cm) from the edge of the paper. Then fold up the bottom diagonal edges along the line where the colors meet.

7 Take the second sheet of paper with the eyes and fold it in half from corner to corner down the middle of the design. Then open out and fold in the side points so that the bottom edges meet along the central crease. Repeat with the upper diagonal edges.

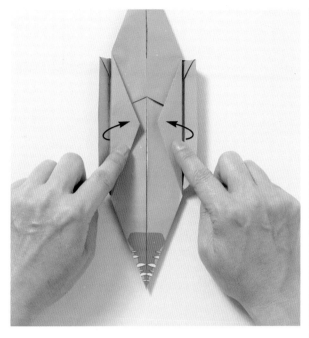

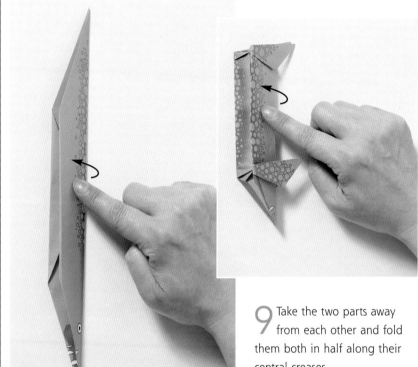

8 Place the second part inside the first and fold over the side points to create vertical edges that match the fold lines inside the first part.

9 Take the two parts away from each other and fold them both in half along their central creases.

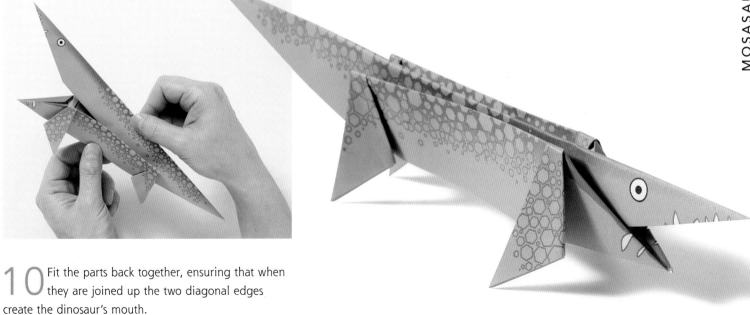

10 Fit the parts back together, ensuring that when they are joined up the two diagonal edges create the dinosaur's mouth.

25 PLESIOSAURUS

The plesiosaurus lived during the early Jurassic period, swimming aound the oceans of northern Europe. It had a small head, long neck, and two pairs of large flippers, which meant it could swim extremely quickly. This model is made by repeating the same folding movements many times so take care when creating its shape and make every crease firm and sharp.

You will need:
One sheet of 12 in (30 cm) square paper

1 Make creases across the paper by folding it in half from side to side both ways, and then from corner to corner both ways, opening it out each time except for the last fold.

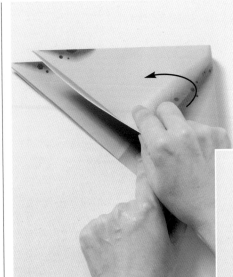

2 Fold the triangle in half along the center crease then lift the top flap and open it, pulling the corner of the paper forward and refolding with a square fold into a diamond shape.

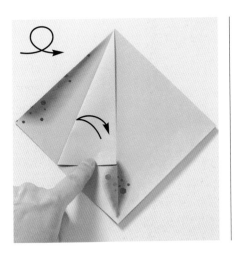

3 Turn the paper over and repeat so that you are left with a diamond shape. Then turn in the left-hand point so that the upper diagonal edge runs down the central crease.

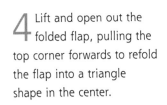

4 Lift and open out the folded flap, pulling the top corner forwards to refold the flap into a triangle shape in the center.

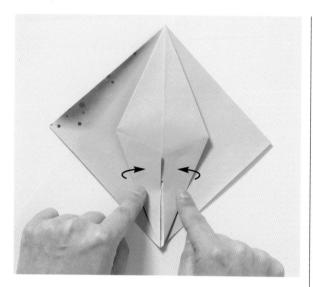

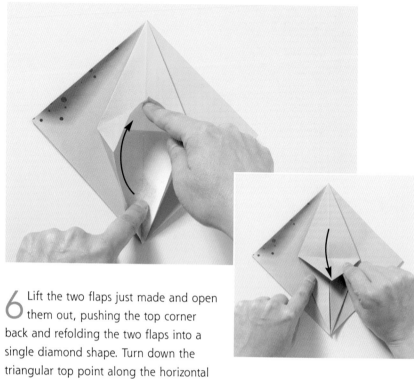

5 Fold over the lower diagonal edges of the flap so that they meet along the central crease, covering all the white area of paper previously showing.

6 Lift the two flaps just made and open them out, pushing the top corner back and refolding the two flaps into a single diamond shape. Turn down the triangular top point along the horizontal crease just made.

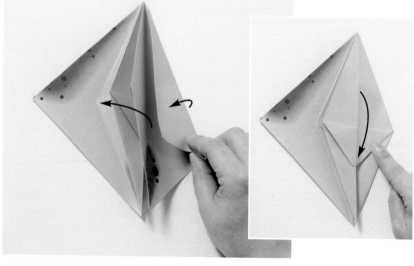

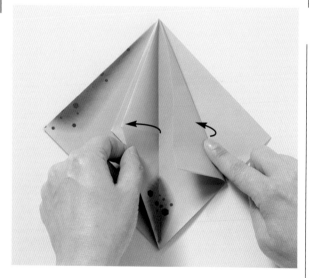

7 Turn the right-hand side of the narrow diamond over the left-hand side and then fold in the upper edge of the next right-hand flap so that it runs down the central crease. Now repeat steps 4–6 to create another narrow diamond shape.

8 Turn over the last flap on the right-hand side and again repeat steps 4–6 so that the only wide flap remaining is on the left-hand side of the model.

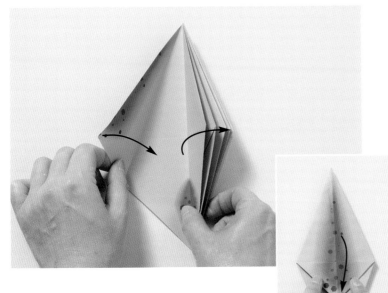

9 Turn all the narrow flaps to the right and fold in the left-hand edge so that it runs down the center line. Again repeat steps 4–6, finishing by turning down the triangular flap in the middle.

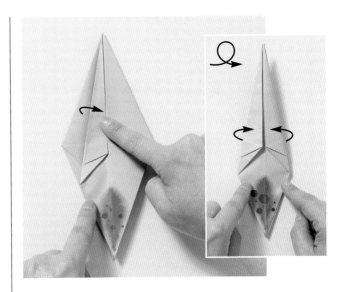

10 Turn over the edges until a flat area of paper is showing. Make sure that there are four flaps on each side of the model. Turn in the upper edges so that they run down the central crease. Turn over the flaps so that you repeat this on all four flat surfaces.

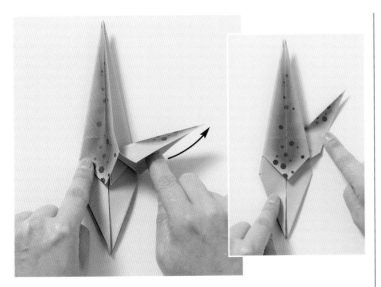

11 Turn over the top flap on the right-hand side so that there are four flaps on each side of the model. Open the right-hand flap slightly and turn up its bottom point, refolding it inside the flap at an angle and pressing down.

12 Now fold the tip down at an angle with the new crease line running inside the flap, then open it up again and fold the tip back inside itself.

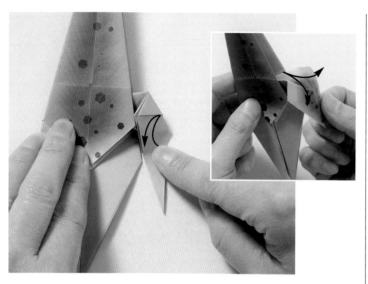

13 Turn the tip down again to make another crease then open it up and fold it outside itself, reversing the direction of the creases and leaving the design showing.

14 Repeat the previous three steps on the other side, so that you are left with two flaps, both of which are pointing downward.

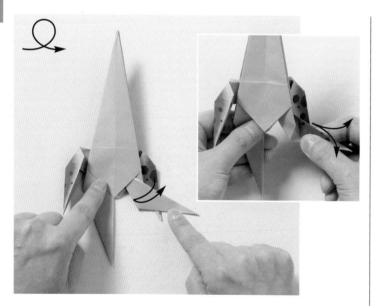

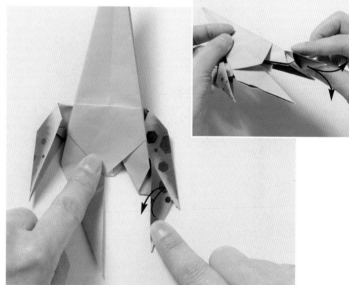

15 Turn the model over and turn up the right-hand flap of the bottom tip, making a diagonal crease line running up inside the model. Open up the flap and reverse the new crease, folding the end of the flap inside itself.

16 As previously, turn the tip over again to make a new crease then open up the flap and turn over the end, making an outside fold with the tip surrounding the flap.

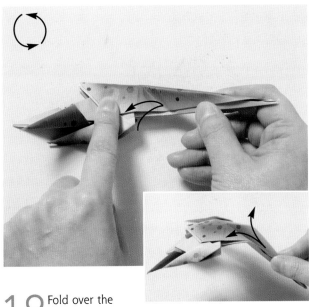

17 Repeat steps 15 and 16 on the other side, so that you are left with all four tips pointing out at an angle and showing the design.

18 Carefully turn over the left-hand side of the model to fold it in half along the central crease.

19 Fold over the long tip at an angle to make a crease, then open up the flap and fold the end inside, reversing the direction of the creases.

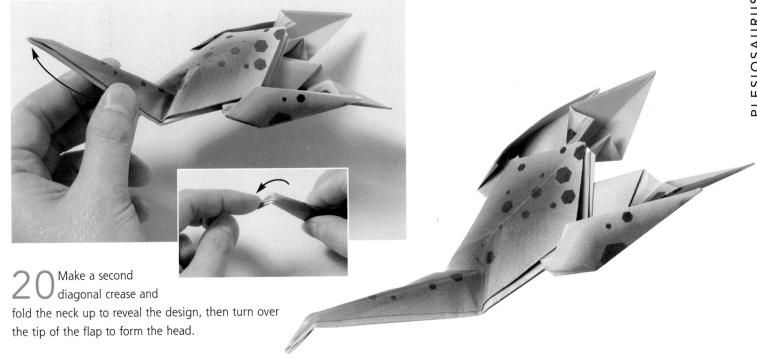

20 Make a second diagonal crease and fold the neck up to reveal the design, then turn over the tip of the flap to form the head.

SUPPLIERS

Origami paper is available at most good paper stores or online. Try searching online for "origami paper" to find a whole range of stores, selling a wide variety of paper, that will send packages directly to your home.

UK
HOBBYCRAFT
Stores nationwide
www.hobbycraft.co.uk
TEL: + 44 (0)1202 596100

JP-BOOKS
www.jpbooks.co.uk
c/o Mitsukoshi, Dorland House
14–20 Regent Street, London SW1Y 4PH
TEL: 020 7839 4839
info@jpbooks.co.uk

JAPAN CENTRE
14–16 Regent St, London SW1Y 4PH
www.japancentre.com
TEL: 020 3405 1150
enquiry@japancentre.com

THE JAPANESE SHOP (online only)
www.thejapaneseshop.co.uk
TEL: 01423 545020
info@thejapaneseshop.co.uk

USA
A.C. MOORE
www.acmoore.com
Stores nationwide
TEL: 1-888-226-6673

CRAFTS, ETC.
www.craftsetc.com
Online store
TEL: 1-800-888-0321

HOBBY LOBBY
www.hobbylobby.com
Stores nationwide

JO-ANN FABRIC AND CRAFT STORE
www.joann.com
Stores nationwide
TEL: 1-888-739-4120

MICHAELS STORES
www.michaels.com
Stores nationwide
TEL: 1-800-642-4235

HAKUBUNDO
www.hakubundo.com
1600 Kapiolani Blvd. Suite 121,
Honolulu, HI 96814
TEL: (808) 947-5503
hakubundo@hakubundo.com

FRANCE
CULTURE JAPON S.A.S.
www.boutiqueculturejapon.fr
101 Bis. Quai Branly 75015, Paris
TEL: + 33 (0)1 45 79 02 00
culturejpt@wanadoo.fr

BOOKS
The Simple Art of Japanese Papercrafts by Mari Ono (CICO Books)
Origami for Children by Mari Ono and Roshin Ono (CICO Books)
Fly, Origami, Fly by Mari Ono and Roshin Ono (CICO Books)
Wild & Wonderful Origami by Mari Ono and Roshin Ono (CICO Books)
Kantan Origami 100 part 2 by Kazuo Kobayashi (Nihon Vogue-Sha Co.Ltd.)
Ugokasu Tobasu Origami by Seibido Shuppan Editorial Department (Seibido Shuppan Co., Ltd.)

WEBSITES
Hiroaki Takai "Origami Kyoshitsu" (Japanese only): www.asahi-net.or.jp/ ~ uz4s-mrym/page/origami0.html
ORIGAMI USA: www.origami-usa.org
British Origami Society: www.britishorigami.info

ACKNOWLEDGMENTS

My big thanks goes to all the team who helped create this book. The very first thank you is to Mr Hiroaki Takai for commissioning, supporting, and advising me on how to make this book a reality.
I've been extremely fortunate in that a great many people have helped me with the book, and to all of them I say a very big thank you. My editor, Robin Gurdon has helped me throughout with his skill and knowledge and I'm also immensely grateful to my photographer, Geoff Dann.
Friends and family have been tremendously supportive, in particular Takumasa, my husband, who has designed all origami papers for this book, and Roshin for his advice. I'd also like to say many thanks to the following: Cindy Richards, Sally Powell, and Pete Jorgensen of CICO Books, as well as Trina Dalziel, who styled and designed the backgrounds for all the projects.